THE LIVERPOOL IVORIES

Joseph Mayer in his Egyptian Museum, c.1856. Detail of portrait by John Harris.
National Museums and Galleries on Merseyside

THE LIVERPOOL IVORIES

LATE ANTIQUE AND MEDIEVAL IVORY AND BONE CARVING IN LIVERPOOL MUSEUM AND THE WALKER ART GALLERY

Margaret Gibson

NATIONAL MUSEUMS & GALLERIES
· ON MERSEYSIDE ·

London: HMSO

© *Crown copyright 1994*
Applications for reproduction should be made to HMSO

ISBN 0 11 290533 1

Designed by HMSO: Alison Beaumont

British Library Cataloguing in Publication Data
A CIP catalogue record for this book
is available from the British Library

HMSO publications are available from:

HMSO Publications Centre
(Mail, fax and telephone orders only)
PO Box 276, London SW8 5DT
Telephone orders 071-873 9090
General enquiries 071-873 0011
(queuing system in operation for both numbers)
Fax orders 071-873 8200

HMSO Bookshops
49 High Holborn, London WC1V 6HB
(counter service only)
071-873 0011   Fax 071-873 8200
258 Broad Street, Birmingham B1 2HE
021-643 3740   Fax 021-643 6510
33 Wine Street, Bristol BS1 2BQ
0272-264306   Fax 0272-294515
9–21 Princess Street, Manchester M60 8AS
061-834 7201   Fax 061-833 0634
16 Arthur Street, Belfast BT1 4GD
0232-238451   Fax 0232-235401
71 Lothian Road, Edinburgh EH3 9AZ
031-228 4181   Fax 031-229 2734

HMSO's Accredited Agents
(see Yellow Pages)

and through good booksellers

Printed in the United Kingdom for HMSO
Dd 294233   C15   3/94   73016

Contents

Foreword

The National Museums and Galleries on Merseyside (NMGM), of which Liverpool Museum and the Walker Art Gallery are two of the principal institutions, was established in 1986. The national status of NMGM rests primarily on the quality and importance of its collections; and one of the most significant of these is the group of ivories collected by Joseph Mayer, a Liverpool goldsmith and antiquarian, the centenary of whose death was also celebrated in 1986. The Liverpool ivories are internationally known and admired and the Trustees of NMGM were clear that their publication was a high priority.

Dr Margaret Gibson, formerly Reader in Medieval History at the University of Liverpool, and now Senior Research Fellow at St Peter's College, Oxford, worked for many years on the ivories in Liverpool Museum and on Joseph Mayer himself. She brought both enthusiasm and an exacting standard of scholarship to the task and this publication is testimony to her determination to complete the project, often under exceedingly difficult circumstances. The Trustees of the NMGM owe Margaret Gibson a considerable debt of gratitude for her work in preparing this publication. I also wish to thank a number of colleagues in NMGM who have assisted with the work over the years, most recently Pauline Rushton, a curator in the Department of Decorative Art, and in particular, Edmund Southworth, head of the Department of Archaeology and Ethnology, who has seen the volume through to publication with HMSO.

The Trustees and HMSO gratefully acknowledge the support of the Marc Fitch Fund towards the publication of this volume.

Richard Foster
Director
National Museums and Galleries on Merseyside

Preface

The Liverpool Free Public Museum was founded in 1851, but its prosperity dates from the 1860s. When the William Brown Library was built in 1857 on the steep slope to the north of St George's Hall, it accommodated not only the original Museum (of which little is known) but two private collections: the Museum of Natural History, formed by the 13th earl of Derby, transferred from Duke Street in 1860, and Joseph Mayer's Egyptian Museum, transferred from Colquitt Street in 1867. Most of the items in the present catalogue are the gift of Joseph Mayer, either in 1867 or in the years immediately following (Introduction ii below). He himself had acquired some of his finest pieces – though by no means all – from the Fejérváry collection (Introduction i below). Further ivories, notably the criophore (No.1), were acquired from various sources in the 1950s and later (Introduction iii below). They are now in the care of the departments of Archaeology and Ethnology (Nos 1–21, 23–6) and Decorative Art (Nos 22, 27–46).

The present catalogue is concerned with the Museum's collection of ivory and bone carvings from the 4th century AD to *c*.1500. A number of earlier items (none of great importance and several of doubtful authenticity) are described by C.T. Gatty in his catalogues of *Egyptian, Babylonian and Assyrian Antiquities* (1879), *Prehistoric Antiquities and Ethnography* (1882) and *Greek, Etruscan and Roman Antiquities* (1883). Some of these early pieces, and many that are discussed here, were displayed in the remarkable Burlington House exhibition of 1923, the anonymous catalogue of which owes a great deal to Margaret Longhurst. Ivory and bone objects from beyond the classical world and medieval Europe – for example Chinese and Afro-Portuguese ivories, of which Mayer had several fine examples – are not included here.

I am grateful to the following institutions for permission to reproduce photographs of items in their care: Hofbibliothek, Aschaffenburg (XIIIa); Benaki Museum, Athens (VIIc); Walters Art Gallery, Baltimore (IIIc, IXh, XXXIb, XXXIIb, XXXVIIIc, XLb, XLIb); Staatsbibliothek, Bamberg (XXVd); Staatliche Museen zu Berlin (IXg, Xb); Museum of Fine Arts, Boston (XLIIc); Museo Civico, Brescia (VIIb); Herzog Anton Ulrich–Museum, Brunswick (XVc); the Cleveland Museum of Art (XLIc); Hessisches Landesmuseum, Darmstadt (XXVIc–f); the Burrell Collection, Glasgow (XXXIVc); Hamburger Kunsthalle, Hamburg (VIb); Kestner Museum, Hanover (XVIIc); the Academy of Arts, Honolulu, (IXd, IXf); the British Library, London (XVb, XXVc); the British Museum, London (VId, XIIIc, XVIId, XLIVb, XLVc); the Victoria & Albert Museum, London (Xc, XXIi, XXVIIb, XXXVb); Bayerisches Nationalmuseum, Munich (IXb); the Metropolitan Museum of Art, New York (XIIIb); Bibliothèque Nationale, Paris (XIVb–c); Musée du Louvre, Paris (XVd, XXVIIIb–c); Stadtbibliothek, Trier (XXVe); Biblioteca Apostolica Vaticana (IIb); Dumbarton Oaks, Washington, DC (Ic).

My principal debts are to Ernst Kitzinger, who read the early entries, to Kathleen Scott, who turned aside from 15th-century English manuscript illumination to provide the basic descriptions of all the Gothic ivories, to Paul Williamson for his help with both the Gothic and the Italian material and to Martin Kauffmann, who read everything several times. I thank the British Academy for a travel grant enabling me to study the Fejérváry papers in Budapest, the curators past and present in the Liverpool Museum for their generosity and patience, and all the friends and colleagues everywhere – particularly in the British Museum – without whom this catalogue could not have been undertaken, and by whose thoughtful advice it has so greatly benefited.

St Peter's College, Oxford
Easter 1993

Plates

4 Romanesque

Introduction

The collection of ivories in the Liverpool Museum has a double origin: those that were purchased as single items by Joseph Mayer c.1830–67 and those that came *en bloc* from the Fejérváry collection in 1855. The latter were part of a much larger and more general collection of antiquities formed in the late 18th and early 19th centuries in northern Hungary.

i. The Fejérváry Collection[1]

Gabor Fejérváry (1781–1851) came from Komlós-Keresztes in the hill country of northern Hungary.[2] It is the land beyond the Tatras mountains, which by the Treaty of Trianon (1920) became part of Czechoslovakia and is now eastern Slovakia. The principal town was Eperies (Prešov), the administrative centre of Saros county, and answerable ultimately to the Habsburg government in Vienna. The family were Lutheran gentry, German-speaking and educated in German, but to some degree conversant with Magyar culture. In the early 19th century the recovery of the Hungarian past – especially the prehistoric and classical past – was an element in the reassertion of Hungarian national identity: it was to be a weapon in the hand of Kossuth and a significant element in the revolution of 1848. In this greater story the Fejérvárys have their part. Gabor's father, Karolì Fejérváry, was a historian and numismatist; he was also a pioneer in the study of prehistoric metalwork, several notable pieces having been found in the locality.[3] Gabor Fejérváry himself frequented the radical salons of Pest, dreaming of the fall of the Habsburgs.[4] Finally his nephew, Ferenc Pulszky, was among the supporters of the revolution who had to flee for their lives in the autumn of 1849.[5] By such a concatenation of chances the Fejérváry ivories were to come to Liverpool.

Gabor Fejérváry never married. He set up house in Eperies and kept an apartment in Pest.[6] He became the family's link with the world beyond Eperies and even – unimaginably – beyond Hungary. 'My uncle Gabor came to visit,' (in 1828, when Ferenc Pulszky was a lad of fourteen or fifteen):

> He had a magnificent marble statue of Venus, several antique bronzes and an outstanding collection of carved gems; there were besides several medieval works of art.[7]

Better still, in 1833 Fejérváry took Pulszky on his first journey abroad: Budapest – Vienna – Milan – Padua – Florence – Rome – Naples, and back home through Venice and Vienna.[8] On that expedition (as Pulszky records) they visited dealers in every city; and when the formal business was done, the talk turned to antiquities. So the Fejérváry collection was built up: in Italy, and on other journeys to France and the German states, and even England.[9]

Man of the world and connoisseur, uncle Gabor dominates the early pages of Pulszky's autobiography. It is easy to see him as a gentleman collector, untroubled by base considerations of finance. But Fejérváry has left his own record, which – if it gives few details of specific acquisitions – conjures up vividly and reliably the milieu in which his collection was formed. Professor Janos Szilágyi of the Fine Arts Museum in Budapest has brought to scholarly attention Fejérváry's *Rechnungs Journal*, his personal account-book for the years 1827–35.[10] This contains anything from a coin given to a beggar to transactions running into hundreds, and occasionally thousands, of florins.[11] Fejérváry emerges as in the first instance a wine merchant, buying and selling Tokay and lesser wines for clients in and beyond Hungary. Serious money changed hands. To what were broadly the same clients Fejérváry would also extend credit.[12] He charged interest to others, raised loans on his own behalf, and negotiated credit for the Pulszkys back in Eperies. His careful record of his own fortunes at whist, month after month, reflects not personal gambling – for the sums involved are trivial – but countless evenings spent with potential clients. Where Fejérváry did take a major risk was in assuming a fifteen-year lease (1830–45) of the opal-mine at Vorösvágás (Czerwenitza), a few miles south-east of Eperies.[13] Although the mine had been badly run for half a century, it was potentially extremely profitable, in that it was still the unique source of good-quality opals known to Europe.[14] (Mexican and Australian opals became available only in the late 1870s.) Initially at least Fejérváry's judgement was vindicated. Income from the sale of opals rose from an already respectable 5,052 florins for the period August 1830–December 1832 to 16,455 florins for 1835 alone.[15]

Scattered through the transactions in wine, the interest on loans, the annual receipts for opals and the multitude of trivia – tobacco, red ink and visits to the theatre – are the only surviving records relating to Fejérváry's purchase of antiquities. Three quarters of the evidence concerns coins, for which he would pay very large sums: 100 florins for a Ptolemaic gold coin.[16] Other antiquities are identified only in the broadest terms: 'three papyrus rolls and 62 bronzes, 225 florins';[17] 'two ivory bas-reliefs, 5 florins'.[18] It is the more surprising suddenly to encounter:

Zwey Dipticha und das fragment von Elfenbein, 2,052 florins.[19]

The diptychs are Asclepius – Hygieia (Nos 5–6) and Clementinus (No.8), for which Fejérváry paid a figure quite out of line with his normal collecting policy, especially for a medium in which he was not primarily interested. Coins and antique bronzes easily took precedence. It may be that Fejérváry had extended credit to Count Mihály Wiczay, from whose family collection both the diptychs came; he would thus have acquired the ivories as the unredeemed pledges on a substantial loan.[20] The same may well be true of the astonishing Mayan codex from pre-Conquest Mexico, which also came from the Wiczay collection.[21]

After 1835, when the account-book ends, the next evidence is an album of drawings, the *Liber Antiquitatis: Fejérvárys Sammlung gezeichnet von Jos. Bucher und Wolfgang Böhm*, made in Eperies in 1842.[22] It consists almost entirely of small antique and oriental bronzes, with not an ivory in sight. In 1844 however Pulszky drew up an inventory of the collection, which includes a detailed account of the ivories: their date and character, their condition, their place of purchase and their price. In the present catalogue this is designated 'Pulszky 1844'.[23] Four years later came the Revolution. In October 1849 Ferenc Pulzsky fled to London, having arranged that on his uncle's death the expected inheritance should be purchased by a third party and by him conveyed to England.[24] Two years later (November 1851) Fejérváry died in Eperies, and his collection (or as much of it as was transportable) duly came to Pulszky.

In 1853 Pulszky's inheritance was exhibited in the rooms of the Royal Archaeological Institute in Suffolk Street, London, with a catalogue prepared by Dr Emeric Henszlmann, an old friend of Fejérváry's, who knew the collection well.[25] This posthumous catalogue (1853) is the only comprehensive review of the Fejérváry collection. In respect of the ivories as such it adds very little to our knowledge,[26] but across the collection as a whole it occasionally indicates the dealers and connoisseurs from whom individual items had been acquired: Denon, Durand and Revil in Paris and a number of private collections across Europe and in England.[27] It was a spectacular display. The old family museum of Hungarica – the coins and prehistoric metalwork – had been transformed into a major collection of classical antiquities. J.O. Westwood, in *The Athenaeum* of July 1853, described the 'collection of carved ivories [as] second only to that possessed by the Bibliothèque Nationale of Paris', devoting several columns to an acute review of the whole spectrum from the Etruscan to the Baroque.[28]

Pulszky had no wish to sell these treasures; but in the spring of 1855 his domestic expenses in London, and his own instinct to go on collecting, led him to offer the ivories to the British Museum. The young A.W. Franks wrote the letter saying that the Trustees had rejected the proposal: 'beyond our means', he ventured.[29] A few months later the money was found by a citizen of Liverpool, Joseph Mayer.[30] In the best traditions of museology Mayer at once commissioned the *Catalogue of the Fejérváry Ivories in the Museum of Joseph Mayer Esq., F.S.A.* (Liverpool, 1856). Pulszky himself prepared the text, one of the first catalogues ever to be devoted entirely to ivories. His introductory essay, in its discursiveness and occasional errors, shows how an intelligent man understood ancient and medieval ivories in the 1850s:[31] the decade when the great London collections were being established, when casts of ivories were first widely available, and when J.O. Westwood and W. Maskell, who were to transform the subject over the next generation, were setting out on their careers.

ii. The Mayer Collection

The story of Joseph Mayer and his collection may be found in a volume published in 1988 by the Society of Antiquaries.[32] Here we need recall only that Joseph Mayer (1803–1886) came from Newcastle-under-Lyme in the heart of Staffordshire. His family on both sides was closely involved with Josiah Wedgwood's factory at Etruria. They were prosperous bourgeoisie, rather than in any sense gentry: Joseph himself came to Liverpool to work in his brother-in-law's shop as a jeweller and goldsmith, and he stayed in the trade all his life. As a collector Mayer had the constant opportunity of purchasing material for his own shop (1844–73) and retaining pieces that specially pleased him. He went on long expeditions to the Continent for business and pleasure, buying for the shop and at the same time augmenting his collection. It is a fair guess that he was offered items of value by sailors, travellers and ship-owners who came into the Port of Liverpool. Mayer had the practical eye of the working jeweller. His sense of classical style he owed to Josiah Wedgwood; his perception of history to William Roscoe and the Royal Institution; and later in life he found a new intellectual home in the Society of Antiquaries. There he dined and talked with the pioneering Roman archaeologist, Charles Roach Smith.[33]

In 1852 Mayer opened his collection to the public at No.8 Colquitt Street, a Regency terraced house in which the two main rooms on the ground floor displayed his extensive Egyptian and classical collection, and smaller rooms upstairs 'medieval and later'.[34] A portrait of *c.*1856 shows him standing in the shadowy grandeur of the Egyptian Room, his hand on an ornate table on which lies the Asclepius – Hygieia diptych (Nos 5–6).[35] The 1850s were the apogee of Mayer's career as a collector, when his museum was crowned with the Faussett collection of Anglo–Saxon antiquities, the Fejérváry ivories and (briefly) the Hertz collection of gems. Eventually however the Colquitt Street Museum exceeded both the physical bounds of a modest Regency house and Mayer's own powers of organisation. In 1867 Mayer gave the entire collection to the town of Liverpool. His munificence is commemorated in a fine statue in St George's Hall.[36] What Mayer did not include was the documentation, specifically his personal records of purchase. The ivories that had not come from the Fejérváry collection appear only in the bare, undated 'Guardbook List' (Concordances ii below), without provenance or date of acquisition. For most other areas of the Mayer collection the position is even worse.

The early curators strove mightily. Eckroyd Smith devised a classification system (Concordances i below), and C.T. Gatty produced four scholarly catalogues, with good illustrations, within five years. Then a great calm fell on the Museum, and the story resumes in the period of reconstruction after the Second World War.

iii. The Twentieth Century

Most of the Liverpool ivories became known to a new generation in the Burlington Fine Arts Club exhibition of 1923 (BFAC). The catalogue of this exhibition – anonymous, but plainly owing much to Margaret Longhurst – has been the basis of subsequent descriptions (e.g. *Liverpool Ivories*) and is still very useful. In the Museum itself Miss Elaine Tankard continued the work of C.T. Gatty. In May 1941 the Museum was hit by an incendiary bomb, which destroyed much of the fabric and some of the contents, particularly in the Department of Decorative Arts. The Museum was closed for a decade.

Among the losses were ten Gothic ivories, all dated to the 14th century, that would no doubt have been included in the present catalogue. They are all described, but not illustrated, in Gatty's catalogue of *Mediaeval and Later Antiquities* (1883):

M 8001   writing tablet: Gatty 62.
          Nativity and Annunciation to Shepherds.

M 8050   diptych: Gatty 59; Koechlin 517.
          Dormition of the Virgin (L) and Crucifixion (R).

M 8058   writing tablet: Gatty 64; Maskell, p.172.
          Crucifixion.

M 8059   writing tablet: Gatty 63; Maskell, p.172; Koechlin 339bis.
          Crucifixion (above) and Entombment (below).

M 8066   diptych panel (R): Gatty 56.
          Crucifixion.

M 8071   diptych panel (R): Gatty 55.
          Crucifixion.

M 8073   diptych: Gatty 52.
          Carrying the cross (L above), Nativity and Annunciation to Shepherds (L
          below); Crucifixion (R above), Adoration of Magi (R below).

M 8074   diptych panel (L): Gatty 54.
          Crucifixion.

M 8076   diptych panel (L): *ex* Rolfe;[37] Gatty 60.
          Dormition of the Virgin: Pl.XLVIII.

M 8077   diptych panel (R): Gatty 61.
          Presentation (L), Crucifixion (R).

From 1950 onwards the collection was refreshed with new acquisitions, most notably the criophore (No.1) from the Castle Museum, Norwich. The Italian bone panels (Nos 44–7) were acquired in 1950, 1953 and 1986; four Gothic ivories (Nos 33–4, 37–8) came from the estate of Philip Nelson in 1953; and a number of late antique furniture panels (Nos 3–4) were bought at auction (1969) and given by the Trustees of the Wellcome Collection (1981). The contentious late Byzantine panels (No.22) were bought in 1986.

iv. The Present Catalogue

The ivory and bone carvings here described are in the Department of Archaeology and Ethnology, if earlier than AD 1200; and in the Department of Decorative Art, if later than AD 1200. All items should be designated 'National Museums and Galleries on Merseyside'.

DEPARTMENT OF ARCHAEOLOGY AND ETHNOLOGY:

1	56.20.330	Criophore.
2	M 10035	Winged youth carrying hare.
3a	1969.111.1	Gladiator fighting a wild animal.

37	53.114.281	Christ with Instruments of the Passion; Nativity and Annunciation to the Shepherds.
38	53.114.280	Writing tablet, showing the Crucifixion.
39	M 8064	Statuette of the Virgin and Child.
40	M 8010	Mirror case, showing an elopement.
41	M 8052	Casket lid, showing tournament with supporting scenes.
42	M 8008–9	Casket panels, showing lovers in conversation.
43	M 8051	Comb, showing Expositor and audience (recto); Fountain of Youth (verso).
44	50.129.1a–d	Four bone panels: the Judgement of Paris.
45	53.114.282a–e; 53.114.283 ab, de	Nine bone panels: Susannah and the Elders.
46	53.114.283c; 50.129.3a–c	Four unrelated bone fragments.
47	1986.227.2	Mirror-frame.

For each item I have given: i. material and measurements – height, width and thickness, in that order; ii. physical condition; iii. a straight description of the imagery; iv. iconography and comparanda; v. bibliography. References (e.g. Koechlin 1285) are to item numbers rather than to pages. Unless otherwise stated items illustrated in colour are shown at actual size.

Colour. Under physical condition, I have briefly noted gilding and colour. For these observations I am much indebted to Dr Carolyn L. Connor, of the University of North Carolina, Chapel Hill, who made a brief, exploratory visit to Liverpool Museum in the spring of 1990. Dr Connor was concerned to identify pieces that would repay further study, rather than to make a definitive report. Technical analysis of the pigments will be required to distinguish original colouring from later additions.[38] In the meantime, we should distinguish gilding from paint. In Late Antique and Byzantine ivories, gilding is more likely than paint to be original;[39] some Anglo-Saxon ivories by contrast may have been painted from the start.[40] Above all, Gothic ivories were often highlighted with gilding and paint.[41]

---

1 I am indebted to Dr Gyöngyi Török, of the National Gallery of Hungary, and Professor Janos Szilágyi, of the Museum of Fine Arts, Budapest, for patient help with the geography and social circumstances of northern Hungary. I am especially grateful to Dr Laszlo Török of the Hungarian Academy for his encouragement to enquire further into the lives of Fejérváry and Pulszky.

2 See the early chapters of F. Pulszky, *Meine Zeit, Mein Leben* (Pressburg / Leipzig, 1880) and E. Henszlmann, 'Levél Fejérváry Gáborról' in *Pulskzy Ferencznek*, ed. N. Jeno et al. (Budapest, 1884), pp.6–11.

3 Most of the manuscripts in the Fejérváry collection were sold by 1830 to Miklós Jankovich (*Meine Zeit* i.45; Henszlmann, p.<2>), from whom they came to the Hungarian National Museum and thus to the Széchényi Library: cf. E. Bartoniek, *Codices Latini Medii Aevi* I (Budapest, 1940), p.v. The prehistoric metalwork came to Liverpool, where much of it was destroyed in the fire of May 1941 (Introduction iii). See S. Nicholson, *Catalogue of the Prehistoric Metalwork in Merseyside County Museums*, University of Liverpool Department of Prehistoric Archaeology Worknotes 2 (Liverpool, 1980), to which add *Liber Antiquitatis* (note 22 below).

4 Pulszky, *Meine Zeit* i.40.

5 See T. Kabdebo, *Diplomat in Exile* (New York, 1979: East European Monographs 56) and, still, Pulszky, *Meine Zeit* iii–iv *passim*.

6 *Rechnungs Journal* (note 10 below): 22 November 1829 and occasional entries concerning furniture thereafter.

7 *Meine Zeit* i.59.

8 Ibid., i.65–99.

9 *Rechnungs Journal* (note 10 below): *passim*, e.g. June–July 1829 in Hamburg, London, Leiden and Amsterdam.

10 Now MS Budapest, Széchényi Library (National Library of Hungary), s.n.

11 The rate of exchange was approximately 12 florins to one pound sterling.

12 The restrictions of feudal tenure in Hungary prevented the aristocracy and gentry, however notionally wealthy, from raising money by the sale of land. This inhibition, combined with the inflation of *c*.1815–30, gave scope for private loans such as Fejérváry extended.

13 S. Butkovic, *Historia Slovenskeho Draheho Opalu z Dubnika* (Bratislava, 1970), p.258; cf. *Meine Zeit* i.41 – where the year is uncertain. I am here greatly indebted to Dr Butkovic's generous help.

14 See most conveniently *Encyclopaedia Britannica* 11th edn (London, 1911), xx.120–1. The international opal-trade has yet to find its historian. Opals remained popular throughout the 19th century (in England until Queen Alexandra declared them unlucky), but nothing is known of how they were distributed. The common belief that they reached Amsterdam via Constantinople derives from Pliny, *Historia Naturalis* xxxvii.80. I am indebted here to the guidance of Shirley Bury of the Victoria & Albert Museum.

15 *Rechnungs Journal*: 1 January 1833 and 31 December 1835.

16 8 July 1828.

17 2 February 1830, to Sturmer. (The papyri were unrolled and expensively framed: 3 April and 20 November 1830.)

18 17 July 1830.

19 8 July 1834; transport of same to Pest 23 August, 4.30 florins.

20 See note 12 above.

21 2 June 1828: 'von Wiczay Elfenbeinerne Becker et Mexicanische Codex, 400F'. There is a complete facsimile of this manuscript (now NMGM, M12014) by C.A. Burland, *Codex Fejérváry-Mayer*, Codices Selecti 26 (Graz, 1971).

22 Budapest, Museum of Fine Arts, Dept of Prints and Drawings, s.n.

23 Széchényi Library, OSzK MS Fol.Germ. 1273, pp.39v–44v.

24 J.G. Szilágyi, in *Pulszky Károly in memoriam*, exhibition catalogue, Museum of Fine Arts (Budapest, 1988), pp.30–43, English summary, pp.137–41, at p.139.

25 *Joseph Mayer*, pp.10–11. Suffolk Street is just west of the National Gallery.

26 Henszlmann, pp.38–41.

27 Henszlmann, *passim*.

28 *The Athenaeum*, no.1343, 23 July 1853, pp.893–4. See also G. Henzen's review, 'Monumenti d'avorio e d'osso', in *Annali del Instituto* 5 (1853), 116–21.

29 'My dear Sir, I fancied that I should have seen you this morning and did not therefore write. I regret to say that the Trustees do not buy the ivories, I suspect on account of the amount, which would certainly have been a heavy pull upon our finances. Ever yours truly, Augustus W. Franks': Széchényi Library, Department of Manuscripts, VIII / 316.

30 Mayer paid 18,000 florins: Pulszky, *Meine Zeit* iii.190.

31 Pulszky returned to Hungary in 1866 to be Director of the National Museum in Budapest. He sold a substantial part of his collection in 1868 (Lugt 30536), a major buyer being the National Museum itself.

32 *Joseph Mayer*, *passim*.

33 Ibid., cap.1.

34 *Joseph Mayer*, pls IV and V.

35 Frontispiece: by John Harris, now in the Williamson Museum and Art Gallery, Birkenhead, no.4566. For Harris see *Merseyside Painters, People and Places*, 2 vols, Walker Art Gallery (Liverpool, 1978), i.110–11, without this portrait.

36   Walker Art Gallery, no.7822.

37   Illustrated in *Publications of the Antiquarian Etching Club* V (1854), pl.46. See section on Losses and Forgeries below.

38   Such analysis has been done on several pieces by the Department of Objects Conservation at the Metropolitan Museum of Art, New York: C.L. Connor, 'New perspectives on Byzantine ivories', *Gesta* 30 (1991), pp.100–111, at p.107. In these cases the pigments appear to be original.

39   A. Cutler, *The Craft of Ivory: sources, techniques and uses in the Mediterranean world, A.D. 200–1400* (Washington, DC, 1985), p.50.

40   See P. Williamson and L. Webster, 'The coloured decoration of Anglo-Saxon ivory carvings', in *Early Medieval Wall Painting and Painted Sculpture in England*, ed. S. Cather, D. Park and P. Williamson, British Archaeological Reports, British Series 216 (Oxford, 1990), pp.177–94.

41   For current enquiry in this field see Williamson and Webster (previous note), p.179, n.13.

1

Late Antique

A library inlaid with ivory and set with glass
Boethius, *De Consolatione Philosophiae* I pr.v.

Ivory was readily available in the late Roman world. At the top end of the market – in senatorial households – it was used for furniture inlay (as in Boethius' library), objects for the table and dressing-room, for ceremonial weapons and for sheer trivia. The criophore (No.1) is such a luxury item. For the less affluent ivory was supplemented or replaced by bone,[1] which served well enough for small objects and decorative inlay, but could not afford an extensive flat surface for serious carving. Whalebone (No.14) seems not to have been an available substitute in antiquity.

But the principal and unique use for ivory in the 4th to 6th centuries AD was the provision of carved diptychs: for consuls and other high officials (Nos 8 and 7 respectively), for the adherents of pagan cults (Nos 5–6), and for representations of Christ and the court of heaven.[2] A diptych consists of two leaves, hinged together to close like a cigarette case. The inner sides are sunken panels, which contained wax (Pl.VIIIb); the outer sides are elaborately carved (Pl.VIIIa). The wax was inscribed with a formal letter of notification or invitation, for instance to the installation of a consul, or to the games that a father would provide for his son's quaestorship. Q. Aurelius Symmachus writes to his brother Flavianus in AD 393: 'I have sent to our lord and prince [the emperor Theodosius I] a diptych framed in gold. Our other friends are honoured with ivory writing-tablets and little silver baskets.'[3] Only the more distinguished guests received their invitations in ivory; lesser men had to be content with terracotta,[4] and less elevated seats in the arena – but the spectacle was not diminished.

The sea-change in the late empire is the 560s and 70s: the loss of half of Italy to the barbarian Lombards, the death of Justinian, the Slav threat to the north and the growing pressure of Persia on the eastern frontier. By 590 a generation of fighting had stabilised the Persian threat. Thirty years later began the seemingly unstoppable expansion of Islam. These political changes coincide with, and in part explain, the sharp decline in the use of ivory in the 7th-century West. From *c*.600–*c*.1300 ivory was virtually unobtainable in the West and not freely available even in the Byzantine East. Then suddenly, in 14th-century Paris, good-quality ivory is back on the market, specialised workshops are established, and a little Gothic diptych is in every self-respecting bourgeois home.

---

1   Nos 2–4; and see Cutler *ibid.*, p.18, fig.20 (the Dumbarton Oaks criophore) *et passim*.

2   The classic corpus of late antique diptychs is Delbrueck. Volbach provides more recent bibliography on Delbrueck's corpus and a good review of the Christian material.

3   Symmachus, *Epp.*ii.81 ('eburneis pugillaribus': ed. O. Seek, Monumenta Germaniae Historica, Auctores Antiqui VI.i (Berlin, 1883), p.66. See also vii.76 (393), p.198, 'to his brothers': 'Offero . . . uobis eburneum diptychum et canistellum argenteum'.

4   See No.7 below.

Plate Ia
Criophore (obverse)

Plate Ib
Criophore (reverse)

1

Criophore

4th century   ?Alexandria

56.20.330

Pls Ia–c

Ivory. 101 × 50 × 25 mm.

The shepherd's L leg is broken off at the knee, and his R hand and forearm are missing. The sheep on his shoulder lacks head and forequarters, formerly pegged into the hole top R. On the back there is a hole towards the top of the tree, and in the base four equidistant holes: in one an ivory peg is still in position, and in another the broken end of a similar peg.

The shepherd carries the sheep across his L shoulder, his R hand holding its rear R leg. He wears a Phrygian cap, a pleated tunic with a decorated hem, and a pouch slung over his R shoulder. Behind him is a tree. Two sheep look up at him, one L (without horns) sitting on its haunches like a dog, one R (with horns) rubbing against the tree. Comparable lamb-bearing shepherds (criophores) are now in Dumbarton Oaks, Washington, DC (Pl.Ic) and the Abegg-Stiftung at Riggisberg, near Bern (Weitzmann 5 and pls iv–v). The Liverpool criophore is the most stylistically rigid: there is little sense of how the weight falls on the shepherd's R leg, or of his spatial relation to the tree, or of the natural height of the seated sheep in relation to its counterpart R. Thence Weitzmann inferred that it was the latest in the group, proposing a date in the 4th century.

The Dumbarton Oaks and Riggisberg criophores are designed to support a weight, whereas the thrust of the Liverpool criophore is towards the base.[1] A useful analogue is the small bone knife-handle in the cantonal museum at Zug (Klauser, p.34 and pl.2f), which was found in an archaeological context of the later 2nd century AD. Free-standing marble statues of the same date (Klauser, pp.35, 45–6), 3rd-century reliefs on sarcophagi (Klauser, pp.37–44) and gold-glass goblet-bases of the 3rd century onwards (Morey 45) indicate the flexibility and persistence of the motif across the Roman world. The primary explanation of the Liverpool criophore is as Orpheus, denoted by his Phrygian cap. The philosophical Christian might see a parallel with Christ, the good shepherd who (like Orpheus) descended to the Underworld: but that is not to imply a Christian patron or to see the criophore as a Christian artefact.

Plate Ic
Dumbarton Oaks criophore. Dumbarton Oaks, Washington, DC

Provenance. Acquired *c.*1880 in the Nile valley by Mr Birkbeck of Thorpe, Norwich, whose widow gave it to the Norwich Museum in 1914. It was sold to the City of Liverpool Museum in 1956.

BFAC 31, pl.I; T. Klauser, 'Studien zur Entstehungsgeschichte der christlichen Kunst I', *Jahrbuch für Antike und Christentum* i (1958), pp.20–51 and pls 1–5, at p.34; A. Legner, *Der gute Hirte* (Düsseldorf, 1959), p.15, fig.6; C.R. Morey, *The Gold-Glass Collection of the Vatican Library, with additional catalogues of other gold-glass collections*, ed. G. Ferrari, Catalogo del Museo Sacro vol.IV (Vatican City, 1959); Weitzmann 5, pp.12–15 and pls iv–v; *Age of Spirituality* 464.

---

1   The pegs in the base indicate that it was fitted to at least two other pieces of ivory, wood, cork or metal. Whether the complete article was purely decorative – a statue on a base – or also functional – e.g. a stopper or the handle of an épergne – we do not know.

Plate IIa
Winged youth carrying hare

2

Winged youth carrying hare

4th century   Egyptian

M 10035

Pls IIa–b

Bone. 174 × 114 × 4 mm.

Incised panel, the lines filled in with mastic, now black. The eye-sockets are drilled holes, now empty. Damaged top L and seriously damaged bottom R; cracks throughout. Stud-holes on R shoulder and both thighs. The two lower studs may have attached a metal skirt concealing the thighs.[1] The main run of 4th–5th-century Egyptian material of this kind is thought to have been mounted on wooden caskets, one complete example of which survives in the Cairo Museum.[2] Individual panels in the same technique survive in a number of major collections,[3] and the tradition itself survived into the 9th century for a last dramatic flowering as the Heracles plaques of the *cathedra Petri* or 'throne of Charles the Bald'.[4]

Winged youth running L to R. He wears a cloak, a long-sleeved tunic, knee-high leggings and laced ankle-boots. He carries a hare in both hands. The ground he runs on is simply indicated; behind him is a crudely-drawn gable. The iconography derives from the personification of October as a man carrying a hare; the design is close to what can be reconstructed of *October* in the Roman calendar of AD 354 (Stern, pl.xi.1: see Pl.IIb). There the rubric, 'Octobri laetus portat uindemitor uuas' and the verses written down the R margin characterise October as the month of the grape harvest.[5] The hare is seen as the traditional enemy of a vineyard (Stern, p.245).

Plate IIb
October, *calendar of AD 354*. Biblioteca Apostolica Vaticana

Henszlmann 658; Pulszky 23; Westwood 13 ('73.12); BFAC 22 and cf. 20–1; J. Strzygowski, *Koptische Kunst: Catalogue Général des antiquités égyptiennes du Musée du Caire* (Vienna, 1904); H. Stern, *Le calendrier de 354: étude sur son texte et sur ses illustrations* (Paris, 1953); *LI* 15; K. Wessel, *Koptische Kunst: die Spätantike in Ägypten*, (Recklinghausen, 1963), pp.195–251, pls 119–27 [appliqué medallions]; K. Weitzmann, 'The Heracles Plaques of St. Peter's Cathedra', *The Art Bulletin* 55 (1973), pp.1–37; L. Marangou, *Bone Carvings from Egypt: I Graeco-Roman period* (Tübingen, 1976), pp.26–7; Randall.

1   See Weitzmann, note 4 below.

2   Strzygowski 7060–4. This casket may not be unique, but complete examples in their original condition are very rare.

3   Athens, Benaki Museum, 10329–30, 18702, 18704, 18707 (Marangou); Baltimore, Walters Art Gallery, 71.40 (Randall 135 and colorplate 44); Cairo Museum, 7065–7, particularly 7067 (Strzygowski, figs 232–4). The British Museum casket (Egyptology, no.5555 [duplicate accession number]), to which reference is made by Strzygowski, pp.174–5, and BFAC no.21, is a roughly-

constructed modern wooden 'casket' (it does not open) made to display two groups of panels found at Memphis; one group is in the relevant technique.

4   Weitzmann, 'Heracles plaques', pp.1–37; note the discussion of metal on ivory (p.24).

5   The rubric reads: 'The joyful vintager carries October's grapes'. The verses culminate in: 'Now froths the bacchic lake, the must pours forth – see how the new wine warms the jar!'.

Plate IIIa
Gladiator fighting a wild animal

Plate IIIb
Nereid

3

Two unrelated panels

1969.111.1–2

Pls IIIa–c

3a

Gladiator fighting a wild animal

4th–5th century   Eastern Mediterranean

1969.111.1

?Ivory. 52 × 104 × 5 mm.

Bas-relief, sunk within an undecorated bevelled frame. R end missing.[1] One hole at the top L corner of the frame and three holes vertically at L extreme of the bas-relief. Regular chisel-marks on reverse.

The gladiator in cloak and tunic, barefoot, opposes his targe to the beast; in his R hand he wields a club. Only the beast's head and paw survive.[2] Tufts of vegetation on the ground at L, centre and R. Such stylised vegetation is common in the incised panels discussed above (No.2) and in illusionist Late Antique manuscript illumination.[3] The classic surviving representation in ivory of such contests between men and beasts is the series of Areobindus diptychs (AD 506).[4]

Provenance. Christie's, London, 4 March 1969, lot 78.

3b

Nereid

4th–5th century   Egyptian

1969.111.2

Ivory. 102 × 58 × 6 mm.

Bas-relief standing clear of plain frame. Reverse scored with close horizontal lines and long crosses (XXX). Damaged top R and bottom L and severely damaged centre L. The dénouement of a scene composed of at least one further panel to the L.

Nereid with a horn in her hair (R), arrows carved on breasts, stomach and thigh, seated in the water. She holds a piece of fruit in her L hand; further such fruit is in a basket above L. Two other figures survive only in their legs: a horse (front legs shown bottom R) and a man, with drapery (R leg across sea-nymph's thigh). The scene may be partially interpreted by analogy with the better-preserved panel in Baltimore (Randall 159 and fig.18: see Pl.IIIc), in which Helios sweeps up in his quadriga.[5] We can infer another figure in a chariot or on horseback skidding to a halt as he reaches the sea-nymph.

Provenance. Christie's, London, 4 March 1969, lot 78.

Strzygowski; L. Marangou, *Bone carvings from Egypt: I Graeco-Roman period* (Tübingen, 1976); Randall.

Plate IIIc
Baltimore casket panel, showing Helios and nereids.
Walters Art Gallery, Baltimore

---

1 For this type of panel see Strzygowski 7070–88 and 7089–7124. Identification of the material of the Liverpool panels by Dr C. Fisher of the National Museums and Galleries on Merseyside.

2 It is worth comparing an equally damaged panel in Cairo: Strzygowski 7112.

3 E.g. Vergilius Romanus: K. Weitzmann, *Late Antique and Early Christian Book Illumination* (London, 1977), no.5.

4 Volbach 8, 10–11.

5 Compare Athens, Benaki Museum 18981, with further references: Marangou 148 and pls 46a (Athens) and 47b (Split).

4
Four miscellaneous bone panels

1981.2111.31–34

Pls IVa–d

The major museums have quantities of such panels, which have not so far had detailed scrutiny. The problems (and opportunities) are well set out by Randall, pp.80–3, who illustrates and catalogues a number in the Baltimore collection.[1] The indispensable study is Marangou's catalogue of the Benaki collection in Athens, which is on a scale that can illustrate the typology of these simple figures: cycles relating to Dionysius and Aphrodite, and – broadly – 'gods and spirits of the Nile'.

Plate IVa
Dancing-girl

Plate IVb
Upper fragment of Dionysius figure

Plate IVc
Urn with vine-scroll

Plate IVd
Shell motif

4a

Dancing-girl

4th–6th century   ?Egyptian

1981.2111.31

Bone. 71 × 38 × 3–4 mm.

Flat panel in which the crudely-executed figure is broadly within the style of the Nilotic art of 4th–6th-century Alexandria (cf. No.3b above). Holes top and bottom centre. The frame lurches from one pattern along the top to another down the sides and a third along the bottom. This stylistic uncertainty has raised doubts as to the authenticity of the piece, doubts which have not been resolved by radio-carbon dating.

Provenance. W.M.A. Reid; sold Sotheby's 17 December 1934, lot 145 to Sir Henry Wellcome; thence Wellcome 156639.

Gibson and Southworth, p.131.

4b

Upper fragment of Dionysius

c.4th century   Egyptian

1981.2111.32

Bone. 80 × 42 × 10 mm.

Curved panel cut in bas-relief, showing a naked youth in a stylised posture that derives from Hellenistic renderings of 'Apollo-Lykeios': Marangou 3 and 10, pls 2a and 5c;[2] cf. Randall 121–3. Radio-carbon dating confirms the authenticity of the piece, giving probable limits of AD 260/430 and virtually certain limits of AD 190/540.

Provenance. As No.4a; Wellcome 156650.

Strzygowski; Randall; Gibson and Southworth, p.131.

4c

Urn with vine-scroll

7th–8th century   ?North Africa

1981.2111.33

Bone. 81 × 36 × 6 mm.

Curved panel carved in fairly high relief; holes top L and bottom R, the latter with its original ?wooden plug. A many-tendrilled plant grows out of an urn.[3] Radio-carbon dating not only confirms the authenticity of the piece, but indicates that it was cut after the Islamic conquest of Egypt (639). The limits are: probable – AD 656/855, virtually certain AD 605/943. The panel thus belongs to a well-defined type of 'abstract plant designs' (Randall, p.82),[4] which were deemed more appropriate than human figures in the new Islamic art.

Provenance. As No.4a; Wellcome 156655.

Strzygowski; Randall; Gibson and Southworth, p.132.

4d

Shell motif

4th century   Egyptian

1981.2111.34

Bone. 34 × 84 × 2–3 mm.

Flat panel, with holes top L and bottom R. The shell is set in a plain rectangular frame. It no doubt stood above the head of a consul or other elevated figure: compare Volbach 3 (Asturius, consul 449), 66, 68 (lovers, poet and muse) and 153–4, 242 (saints).

Provenance. As No.4a; Wellcome 156656.

---

1   See also Strzygowski 7089–7124.

2   Athens, Benaki Museum 18904 and 18900. See comprehensively Marangou, pp.31–2, with references, and pls 1–10.

3   Cf. Strzygowski 8865–7, figs 263–5.

4   Cf. Randall 217a–c.

5–6

Asclepius – Hygieia diptych

*c.*AD 400–30   Rome

M 10044

Pls V–VI, VIa–d

Ivory. *Asclepius* (L) 314 × 139 × 6 mm.;
Hygieia (R) 314 × 139 × 6–7 mm.

The L panel (Asclepius) has three hinge-holes on the R edge. Upper L badly damaged; top R corner broken off and glued into place; upper R edge damaged. The reverse is a sunken panel within an outer frame *c.*5 mm. across, in the manner of a consular diptych. Traces of gold on both arms, of orange-red pigment in the centre of the body and of green crystals in the fold of the cloak. On the reverse blue pigment top R.

The R panel (Hygieia) has one hinge-hole on L edge; the lower two are lost by damage lower down L edge. Centre L badly damaged; upper L (along a line from the centre of the *tabula ansata* through the snake to above R of Eros' head) crudely rivetted into place: two surviving copper or brass rivets above the snake and two rivet-holes above Eros; a line of four small holes below the *tabula ansata*. The frame is canted slightly inwards. Traces of gold behind the head of the snake top R, of orange-red pigment on Hygieia's hair, of red in R border and on R-hand draped wreath and of green in R border. Medieval or later writing on reverse, now illegible.

The diptych. Statue of Asclepius, with Telesphorus on his R, set on a plinth and in a frame with foliate ornament. Asclepius stands leaning on a rough-hewn staff; his robe leaves bare the R shoulder and chest; he wears sandals. In his L hand is a roll. A male snake (bearded) coils up his staff; in front of the staff (bottom R) is an oxhead (*boucranion*). The child Telesphorus stands bottom L, hooded and displaying an open scroll. The figures are framed by two columns linked by swags of oak-leaves; the top of the L column is missing, on the R column a basket of roses and laurel. The semicircle halfway down the R frame may be a vestige of the *omphalos*, the stone at Pergamon that was honoured as the centre or navel of the world. The *tabula ansata* above, Telesphorus' scroll and the plinth below are all blank, with no sign that inscriptions have been erased. A possible explanation is a painted inscription (Delbrueck, p.215; Cameron, p.400).

Plates V–VI (opposite page)
Asclepius – Hygieia diptych. (Reduced)

Statue of Hygieia, with Eros on her R, set on a plinth and in a frame with foliate ornament. She leans her L elbow on a tripod, her L foot on the tripod's base. She is wearing a long-sleeved dress over another long garment, sandals and a metal circlet on her head. She offers an egg to a female snake (beardless), which coils through the tripod and round her shoulders. Eros wears a cloak and holds a bow in his L hand. The figures are framed by two columns linked by swags of

Plate VIa
Statue of Asclepius and Telesphorus in the Palazzo Massimi, Rome. Archivi Alinari, Florence

oak-leaves; on the L column a child lets a snake out of a basket (the so-called *cista mystica*), on the R column a paten and a jug with a snake coiling round it. The *tabula ansata* above and the plinth below are both blank, as in the Asclepius panel.

The cult. The cult of Asclepius, long current in the Greek world (Kerényi), came to Rome in 293 BC, in response to an epidemic in the city.[1] Tradition had it that a snake was sent from Epidauros; it escaped onto the *isola tiberina*, and there the Roman cult was established. By the 1st century AD a string of oxheads (*boucrania*), culminating in a bust of Asclepius, had been cut in the wall that reinforces the south side of the island.[2] The statue of Asclepius within the temple is described by Ovid:

> . . . just as he always looks in his temple: in his left hand a staff with the bark still on it, his right hand pulling at the hair of his long beard. (*Metamorphoses* xv.654–6)

The statue on the diptych is a type of about a century later (Kerényi III),[3] approximately contemporary with the series of coins issued (AD 139–47) by Antoninus Pius to commemorate the origins of Rome; the Asclepius coin, showing the serpent arriving at the *isola tiberina*, is seventh in the series.[4] The public cult was still active in the 4th century: it appears for example in the Filocalus kalendar of 354.[5] By the mid-5th century however the *isola tiberina* was a prison,[6] though the healing shrine may have persisted in association with the 6th-century church of San Bartolomeo in isola.

As to the cult of Hygieia, the assumption has always been that she accompanied Asclepius, either in her own name or as Salus.[7] But both specific notices of her cult and surviving statues are very rare;[8] and it may be thought that she only really came into her own in the philosophical stage of the cult of Asclepius – Hygieia, to which we now turn.

The context. In its evocation of the old religion Asclepius – Hygieia invites comparison with the group of ivory panels commissioned by the Symmachi in the first quarter of the 5th century (Cameron):[9] the Symmachorum – Nicomachorum diptych of 402, the closely related panel that was later recut for the otherwise unknown ENNOBERTUS,[10] and the *Consecratio* panel showing the apotheosis of an emperor.[11] The Asclepius – Hygieia diptych cannot be related in the same way to a specific family; it may best be understood in the context of Macrobius' *Saturnalia*. This philosophical symposium was written *c*.430, but it is set in the 370s, in the last generation of the public observance of the pagan cults.[12] In

the passage that follows Praetextatus explicates the cult of Asclepius and Salus (otherwise Hygieia):

> Statues of Aesculapius and Salus have snakes at their feet, because they relate to the sun and the moon. Aesculapius is that beneficial strength from the sun's very being which maintains the bodies and souls of mortal men. Salus is the influence of the moon, whereby the bodies of all living creatures are strengthened with good health. They are shown with snakes at their sides because they cause our human bodies to put off the skin of weakness and recover their original strength, just as every year snakes put off the skin of old age and so renew their vigour. The sun itself is like a snake, for it returns continually from the depth of age upwards to recover its youthful strength . . . Indeed (Praetextatus continues) Aesculapius *is* Apollo, both as his son and as sharing his gift of divination. In the same way a doctor making a prognosis of health or sickness perceives 'quae sint, quae fuerint, quae mox uentura sequentur'. (*Georgics* iv.393)[13]

Whether or not the historical Praetextatus actually wrote or thought in this manner, for Macrobius and the literary and philosophical circles in Rome *c*.430 this was the only way in which the old cults could still make sense: as visible correlates of the syncretic neo-Platonism of the day. The Asclepius – Hygieia diptych belongs not to the public cult of the 370s, but to a circle within the Roman intelligentsia in the early 5th century, for whom it was an icon of the philosophy to which they adhered and by which they tried to live.

The provenance. Exceptionally we have the provenance from *c*.1500, when an unknown artist made sketches of twentyone items in the Gaddi collection in Florence.[14] Asclepius and Hygieia are at the extreme top R of his page of drawings (Pl.VIb). The diptych remained with the Gaddi family until the 1750s, when their collection was at least partly dispersed; the manuscripts were sold in 1755.[15] In the mid-18th century it was displayed in a fine marquetry box (Pl.VIc), which is a careful rendering of both panels.[16] It departs from the evidence at only two points: in supplying a cock to complete the damaged top L corner of the Asclepius panel,[17] and in providing inscriptions for the *tabulae ansatae* and the plinths. The cock refers to the last words of Socrates: 'We owe a cock to Aesculapius – see that it is paid' (Phaedo 118). The first inscription runs: M.AVR.ANTONINUS P.F.AVG. (above Asclepius) P.M.TR.P.XVIII.COS.IIII.P.P. (above Hygieia). The source is a bronze sestertius of Caracalla for the year AD 215 (Pl.VId).[18] The obverse has the inscription as quoted, and the reverse shows Asclepius with his staff and the child Telesphorus. Such a coin had figured in the literature on Asclepius since the late 17th century;[19] thus whoever designed the marquetry box knew where to look. The second inscription runs: AESCVLAPIO HYGIAE (Asclepius's plinth) TELESPHORO

Plate VIb
Asclepius and Hygieia (top right) *among drawings of items in the Gaddi collection, c.1500.*
Hamburger Kunsthalle, Hamburg

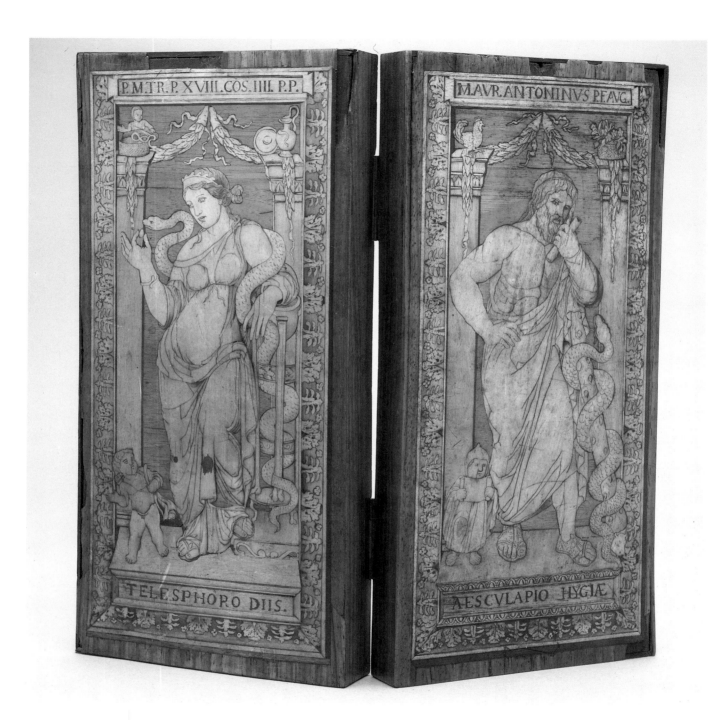

P.M.TR.P.XVIII.COS.IIII.P.P.

TELESPHORO DIIS.

M.AVR.ANTONINVS P.F.AVG.

AESCVLAPIO HYGIÆ

Plate VIc
Marquetry box to contain Asclepius – Hygieia diptych.
National Museums and Galleries on Merseyside

Plate VId
Sestertius of Caracalla, AD 215 (obverse and reverse).
Trustees of the British Museum, London

DIIS (Hygieia's plinth). It needs no special explanation. By c.1800 the diptych was with Caronni,[20] who sold it to Count Mihály Wiczay of Hédervár in south-west Hungary. Wiczay in turn sold it to Fejérváry in 1834.[21]

B. de Montfaucon, *L'Antiquité expliquée et représentée en Figures* I.ii (Paris, 1719); Gori iv.62–4, pls xx–xxi; Pulszky 1844, Roman 1; Henszlmann 656; Pulszky 25–6; Waring, Sculpture, pl.1.1 (Hygieia); Maskell, pp. 165–7; Westwood 15–16 ('54.45–46'); Meyer (1879) 55; M. Besnier, *L'Ile tibérine*

dans l'antiquité, Bibliothèque des Écoles Françaises d'Athènes et de Rome 87 (Paris, 1902); A. Maskell, *Ivories* (London, 1905), pl.X; H. Graeven, 'Heidnische Diptychen', *Mitteilungen des deutschen archäologischen Instituts*, Römische Abteilung 28 (1913), pp.198–304, at 220–43; BFAC 24; Delbrueck 55; *LI* 11; C. Kerényi, *Asklepios: archetypal image of the physician's existence* (London, 1960); *MRT* 99; Volbach 57; *Age of Spirituality* 133; Gaborit-Chopin, p.21 (fine colour plate); A. Cameron, 'A new late antique ivory: the Fauvel panel', *American Journal of Archaeology* 88 (1984), pp.397–402 and pls.55–6; *Spätantike* 222.

---

1 Livy, *Ab urbe condita* x.48.

2 Still partly visible: Kerényi, pl.2; and see Piranesi, *Veduti di Roma* II.121 (Rome, 1751); H. Focillon, *Giovanni-Battista Piranesi: essai de catalogue raisonné de son oeuvre* (Paris, 1918), no.836 (121).

3 The best analogy is the statue now in the Palazzo Massimi alle Valle in Rome (Pl.VIa): see J. Spon, *Miscellanea eruditae antiquitatis* (Lyons, 1685), pp 312–13, no.III; D. de Rossi, *Paolo Alessandro Maffei: Raccolta di Statue Antiche e Moderne* (Rome, 1704), col.124–6 and pl.cxxxii; B. de Montfaucon, *L'Antiquité expliquée et représentée en figures*, 5 vols (Paris, 1719), I.ii.286 and pl.clxxxvii (repeating de Rossi's drawing).

4 The Asclepius coin was issued AD 140/144. See Kerényi, pl.8; J.C. Toynbee, *Roman Medallions*, American Numismatic Society (New York, 1944), p.143.

5 11 September, 'N<atalis> Asclepii': Th.Mommsen, *Inscriptiones Latinae Antiquissimae* I, 2 edn, *CIL* i (Berlin, 1893), p.272.

6 Sidonius, *Epp.*I.vii.12: Capite multatus in insulam coniectus est serpentis Epidauri (AD 469).

7 Vitruvius, *De architectura* I.ii.7; Macrobius, *Saturnalia* I.xx.1–4. (see below).

8 A relevant survivor is the statue of Hygieia and Eros formerly at Lowther castle: A. Michaelis, *Ancient Marbles in Great Britain* (Cambridge, 1882), p.490, no.4.

9 Cameron argues persuasively that the Nicomachorum panel commemorates Virius Nicomachus Flavianus (*ob*.394) and the Symmachorum panel Q. Aurelius Symmachus (*ob*.402). The commissioning patron would be the latter's son, Q. Fabius Memmius Symmachus.

10 Now lost, but carefully reproduced by Montfaucon, *L'Antiquité expliquée* II.i, pl.83. This panel was brought to scholarly attention by P. Lasko, 'An unnoticed leaf of a late antique ivory diptych, and the temple of Mercury in Rome', *The Vanishing Past: studies of medieval art, liturgy and metrology presented to Christopher Hohler*, ed. A. Borg and A. Martindale, BAR

International Series 111 (Oxford, 1981), pp.89–94, pls 7.1–3. See further Cameron, *passim*.

11 Now London, British Museum, MLA 57.10–13.1 (Volbach 56).

12 Macrobius' *dramatis personae* are: Q. Aurelius Symmachus (*ob*.402), Virius Nicomachus Flavianus (*ob*.394), V. Agorius Praetextatus (*ob*.380) and, all early 5th century, Avienus, Caecina Albinus, Furius Albinus and Servius the Grammarian.

13 *Saturnalia* I.xx.1–4. Modern editors of Virgil prefer 'trahantur'.

14 Hamburger Kunsthalle Kupferstichkabinett Inv.No.21205; analysis by G. Pauli, *Zeichnungen alter Meister in der Kunsthalle zu Hamburg: Italiener*, XIII Veröffentlichung der Prestel-Gesellschaft (Frankfurt-am-Main, 1927), pl.15. The attribution to the Gaddi collection depends on Pauli, no.15, a marble altar that is known to have been in their ownership; see further Molinier i.42–3.

15 M. Parenti, *Aggiunte al Dizionario Bio-bibliografico . . . di Frati*, 2 vols (Florence, 1959), ii.106.

16 See the Harris portrait of Joseph Mayer (frontispiece). The box was lined with leather, to which the panels were glued: cf. Delbrueck, p.215.

17 Gori's *Thesaurus* shows a second basket of fruit as the missing element top L; but the artist may simply have borrowed this from the Hygieia panel.

18 H. Mattingly, *Coins of the Roman Empire in the British Museum* V, 2 edn (London, 1975), Caracalla 278 (obverse), 279 (reverse).

19 Jacob Spon published a similar coin for the year 214, inscribed TR.P.XVII rather than (as on coins of 215 and on the box) TR.P.XVIII: *Recherches curieuses d'antiquité* (Lyons, 1683), p.533. Montfaucon referred in passing to 'une medaille de Caracalla', without illustrating it: *L'Antiquité expliquée* I.ii, p.286.

20 <F. Caronni> Barnabita, *Ragguaglio di alcuni monumenti di antiquità ed arti* (Milan, 1806), pp.201–65, pls.ix–x.

21 *Rechnungs Journal*, 8 July 1834.

Plate VIIa
Venatio. (Reduced)

7

Venatio

Early 5th century   Rome

M 10042

Pls VIIa–c

Ivory. 294 × 120 × 6 mm.

L panel of a diptych. Two slots for hinges on verso of R edge; above the upper slot a pair of holes (visible top R) and below the lower slot a matching pair (bottom R) with two ivory pins still in place, the upper one visible on the recto. Two further holes on R edge; two more top centre (at head of central figure). A third pair of holes bottom R. The verso is a sunken panel to hold wax, within an outer frame. At the top, eleven lines of post-medieval German text in ink, little now being legible. Traces of blue pigment on the balcony and of gilding on the lower edge.

Three men of senatorial rank, all wearing togas, sit on a balcony watching a stag-fight in the arena below. The young man in the centre displays a silver dish in his R hand; on the L an older man gestures towards the honorand in the centre, on the R the third man holds in his R hand a *mappa* to start the display below. The balcony has four herms (human heads on pillars)[1] and alternating panels of solid and *à jour* carving;[2] in the angles below are two dolphins. The stag-fight features two animals and four *venatores* (literally, huntsmen).[3] The first enters from L, charges at one of the fighters from R, attacks the principal fighter from L and is fatally wounded with a pike, and finally lies dying on the sand below. The second stag enters from R, as though to exit again through the L-hand door. Four fighters take part, all wearing short tunics and leggings: an older man top R, two lads top L and bottom R, and the principal fighter (centre R), who is on a larger scale than his three associates. Four doors; on the door bottom R a life-size engraving of a fighter clad in a loin-cloth. Acanthus border with narrow, plain frames inside and outside. The outer frame on the R is broken away centre and below, doubtless due to the succession of devices attaching this panel to its lost neighbour.

Given Theodosius' legislation of 384 prohibiting the use of ivory for non-consular diptychs, this panel is likely to have been cut in Rome rather than in Constantinople.[4] The honorand (top centre) presides over games marking his quaestorship.[5] It has been persuasively argued that the venue

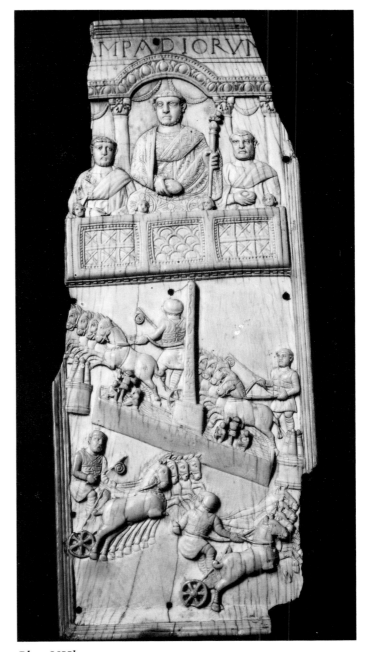

Plate VIIb
Lampadiorum *diptych panel.* Museo Civico Cristiano, Brescia

is the Colosseum itself, the three patrons being seated at podium level, perhaps in the consul's box on the east side of the arena.[6] By contrast, the Lampadiorum / Rufiorum diptych (of which only the Lampadiorum wing now survives: Pl.VIIb) is set in the Circus Maximus.[7] The patrons of the *Venatio* cannot be identified. As to the date, there are three arguments in favour of the first quarter of the 5th century. Stylistically the stags are carved with a fluency more characteristic of the earlier 5th century than later on. Legally the classic gladiatorial fight to the death between men was prohibited in the West in 325 by Constantine.[8] Fights between men and animals were an acceptable and exciting substitute. Finally in the humble medium of terracotta there is an analogue to *Venatio*, found in North Africa, possibly from Carthage.[9] Showing three senators (of which the larger central figure may be compared with the *Lampadiorum* panel: note 7 above) in a balcony with the herms and *à jour* carving of the *Venatio* panel, this is probably an event in the Colosseum. It confirms the type of model available in the western empire, *c.*AD 400.

Provenance. The *Venatio* panel first comes to light in P.G. de Roujoux's collection at Macon in 1804 (Millin i.400–3, pl.xxiv, no.3). Thereafter it passed to Vivant Denon in Paris, and so via Bruno Denon to Fejérváry.

A.L. Millin, *Voyage dans les Départements du Midi de la France*, 4 vols (Paris, 1807–11); Pulszky 1844, Roman 2; Henszlmann 657; Pulszky 27; Waring, Sculpture, pl.I.3; Maskell, pp.167–8; Meyer 41; Westwood 37 ('54.49); A. Maskell, *Ivories* (London, 1905), pl.V.1; BFAC 25; E. Maclagan, 'An undescribed early Christian ivory diptych', *Antiquaries Journal* 3 (1923), pp.99–117; Delbrueck 58; L. Robert, *Les Gladiateurs dans l'orient grec*, Bibliothèque de l'École des Hautes Études 278 (Paris, 1940), pp.324–31; R. Delbrueck, 'Zu spätrömischen Elfenbeinen des Westreichs', *Bonner Jahrbücher* 152 (1952), pp.165–89, at 179–80, pls.27–36, at pl.27; LI 12; H. Wrede, *Die spätantike Hermengalerie von Welschbillig* (Berlin, 1972); J.W. Salomonson,

Plate VIIc
Terracotta fragment, showing spectators at games.
Benaki Museum, Athens

'Kunstgeschichtliche und iconographische Untersuchungen zu einem Tonfragment der Sammlung Benaki in Athen', *Bulletin antieke Beschaving* 48 (1973), pp.3–82, at pp.14–17, figs 7–9; Volbach 59; *Age of Spirituality* 84 and cf.83; *Spätantike* 222.

1　Wrede, pp.131–2 and pl.73.3.

2　That is, the effect shown is *à jour*; the *Venatio* panel itself is not perforated.

3　Maclagan, p.103, n.3, argues for three animals, the one at the top being already dead.

4　*Codex Theodosianus* XV.9.1 (Theodosius I: 25 July 384).

5　The legal onus on senators to provide entertainment and largesse when their children assumed public office is well documented for the 4th and early 5th centuries in both parts of the Empire. Symmachus' provision for his son is noted above.

6　S.B. Platner and T. Ashby, *A Topographical Dictionary of Ancient Rome* (Oxford / London, 1929), pp.6–11. That the *Venatio* panel relates to the Colosseum rather than the Cynegion in Constantinople may be argued from the details of the structure of the Colosseum – its podium, its bronze balustrade –

contrasted with what we know of the Cynegion as portrayed on the base of the column of Theodosius in the Hippodrome: A. Chastagnol, *Le sénat romain sous le règne d'Odoacre: recherches sur l'epigraphie du Colosée au Ve siècle*, Antiquitas in 4o III (Bonn, 1966), pp.57–9. See also G. Egger, 'Die Architekturdarstellung im spätantiken Relief' in *Jahrbuch der Kunsthistorischen Sammlungen in Wien* 55 (1959), pp.7–30, at pp.18–19.

7　Volbach 54. The patrons on their balcony should be compared with *Venatio*, even to the similar panelling on the balcony and the four small heads, which may or may not be herms – they are curiously detached from the pillars below (but see Wrede, pp.131–2). In ivory the only other surviving animal-fight of any quality is the fine lion-hunt now in St Petersburg (Volbach 60).

8　Theodosian Code 15.12.1; Justinian, *Codex* XI.44 (repeats Constantine).

9　Now Athens, Benaki Museum, 12427. See Salomonson, pp.12–20 and fig.7.

8

Clementinus diptych

AD 513   Constantinople

M 10036

Pls VIIIa–b

Ivory. Each panel 370 × 125 mm. (thickness not measurable within frame).

Two hinge-sockets at centre and lower L of L panel, and centre and lower R of R panel. L column on L panel damaged at top. Verso of both panels sunk to contain wax. The panels are mounted in reverse order in a marquetry frame of probably the later eighteenth century. Thus on the recto the panel inscribed FL.TAVRVS CLEMENTINVS etc. should be on the R, on the verso the Greek prayer should read + ΣΤΟΜΕΝ ΚΑΛΟΣ.

Recto: L panel. Clementinus as consul, seated on a stool with lion-heads and lions' feet, the cushion and seat shown face-on, rather than in perspective; the consul's feet on a two-tiered footstool. In Clementinus' R hand the *mappa* to start his consular games, and in his L hand a sceptre with the emperor's head on top. To the L the figure of Constantinople, to the R the figure of Rome, each standing in front of a Corinthian column. Above the consul's head the Greek monogram ΚΛΕΜΗΝΤΙΝΟΥ; and on the *tabula ansata* above the Latin inscription + FL. TAVRVS. CLEMENTINVS. / ARMONIVS. CLEMENTINVS. + . Medallions of the empress Ariadne (L) and the emperor Anastasius (R) above, with a cross between. In the lower part of the panel, beneath the stool and footstool, two barefooted youths pour out largesse: two sacks of coins, with ingots and silver laurel leaves.

R panel. Iconographically identical with L panel. The Latin inscription reads: + V[IR] IL[LVSTRIS]. COM[ES]. SACR[ARVM]. LARG[ITIONVM]. EX CONS[VL]. / PATRIC[IVS]. ET CONS[VL]. ORDIN[ARIVS]. + . Minor stylistic differences include: crosses above the capitals on the columns incised rather than in bas-relief; Rome's R earring shown; different patterns on seat of stool; different decoration on both tiers of footstool; six silver dishes among the largesse. This is the sole evidence that Clementinus was 'comes sacrarum largitionum'; his honorary consulship, patriciate and consulship are attested elsewhere.[1]

Verso. The R panel has an unexplained DO in the upper border. The text consists of an excerpt from the Greek liturgy,[2] a prayer for John, priest of St Agatha, and (in another hand) prayers on behalf of Pope Hadrian I, Andrew Machera and John the priest. First prayer:

+ ΣΤΟΜΕΝ. ΚΑΛΟΣ / + ΣΤΟΜΕΝ ΕΥΛΑΒΟΣ / + ΣΤΟΜΕΝ ΜΕΤΑ ΦΟΒΟΥ / ΠΡΟΣΧΟΜΕΝ ΤΙ ΑΓΙΑ ΑΝΑΦΟΡΑ / ΕΝ ΙΡΙΝΗ ΤΩ Θ(Ε)Ω ΠΡΟΣΦΕΡΕΙΝ / ΕΛΕΩΣ ΕΙΡΙΝΗ / ΘΥΣΙΑ ΑΙΝΕΣΕΩΣ / Η ΑΓΑΠΙΤΟΥ Θ(ΕΟ)Υ ΚΑΙ Π(ΑΤ)Ρ(Ο)Σ / ΚΑΙ Η ΧΑΡΗΣ ΤΟΥ Κ(ΥΡΙΟ)Υ ΚΑΙ Θ(ΕΟ)Υ / ΚΑΙ Σ(ΩΤΗ)Ρ(Ο)Σ ΗΜΩΝ Ι(ΗΣΟ)Υ Χ(ΡΙΣΤΟ)Υ / ΕΦ ΗΜΑΣ ΑΜΗΝ.

Let us stand with dignity, *stand in reverence*, stand in awe. Let us attend with the holy offering, to present it to God in peace. Mercy and peace: the sacrifice of praise. *The <...> of the loving God and Father and the grace of the Lord and God and our Saviour Jesus Christ <be> upon us.*

Prayer for John, priest of St Agatha:

ΜΝΗΣΘΗΤΙ Κ(ΥΡΙ)Ε ΤΟΥ ΔΟΥΛΟΥ / ΣΟΥ ΙΩΑΝΝΟΥ ΕΛΑΧΙΣΤΟΥ / ΠΡΕΣΒΥΤΕΡΟΥ ΜΟΝΗΣ ΤΗΣ Α / ΓΙΑΣ ΑΓΑΘΗΣ ΑΜΗΝ.

Remember O Lord your servant John, humblest priest of the monastery of St Agatha, Amen.

Text added in another hand:

Τ Α ΕΤΙ ΑΔΡΙΑΝΟΥ ΠΑΤΡΙΑΡΧ(ΟΥ) ΠΟΛ(ΕΩΣ)
In the first year of Hadrian, patriarch of the city (R panel, at the end of the prayer).
+ ΜΝΗΣΘΗΤΙ Κ(ΥΡΙ)Ε ΤΟΥ ΔΟΥΛΟΥ ΣΟΥ ΑΝΔΡΕΟΥ ΜΑ / ΧΕΡΑ
Remember thy servant Andrew Machera (R panel, below).
+ ΜΝ(ΗΣΘΗΤΙ) Κ(ΥΡΙ)Ε ΤΟΥ ΔΟΥ(ΛΟΥ) Κ(ΑΙ) ΠΥΜΕΝ(ΟΣ) ΙΜΟΝ ΑΔΡΙΑΝΟΥ ΠΑΤΡΙΑΡΧΟΥ
Remember, Lord, thy servant and our shepherd, Hadrian the patriarch (R panel, below, written vertically).
+ ΜΝΙΣ(ΘΗΤΙ) Κ(ΥΡΙ)Ε / ΤΟΥ ΔΟΥ(ΛΟΥ) / ΙΩΑΝΝ(ΟΥ) / ΑΜΑΡ(ΤΩΛΟΥ) / ΠΡ(ΕΣ)Β(ΥΤΕΡΟΥ).
Remember [thy] servant John, sinner [and] priest (L panel, below, L column, written vertically).
+ Ι ΑΓΙ / Α
The holy (L panel, below, second column, written vertically).
+ ΘΕΩΤΩΚΟΣ
Mother of God (L panel, below, third column, written vertically).
+ Ι Α / ΓΙ / Α
The holy (R panel, below, second column, written vertically).
+ ΑΓΑΘΗ
Agatha (R panel, below, third column, written vertically).

This additional text may be dated to the late 8th century, Hadrian being pope 772–95.

Recto. Fl.Taurus Clementinus was eastern consul in 513. When the panels are set in their original order (so that the hinge-slots match), the inscription on the *tabulae ansatae*

Plate VIIIa
Clementinus diptych (obverse). (Reduced)

ΚΑΛΟС
ΕΥΛΑΒΟС
ΜΕΤΑΦΟΒΟΥ
ΤΙΑΓΙΑΑΝΑΦΟΡ
ΘωΠΡΟСΦΕΡΕΝ
ΕΙΡΙΝΗ
ΑΙΝΕСΕωС
ΚΑΙΠΡС
ΤΟΥΚΥΚΑΙΘΥ
ΙΥ ΧΥ
ΑΜΗΝ
ΤΟΥΔΟΥΛΟΥ

ΕΛΑΧΙСΤΟΥ
ΜΟΝΗСΤΗСΑ
ΑΜΗΝ

ΛΟΥСΟΥΑΝΔΡΕΟΥΜΑ
ΚΕΡΑ   ✝ΑΠ
          ΛΟ
✝ΜΝΙСΛ
ΤΟΥΛΟΥ
ΓωΑΝΗ
ΑΜΑ
ΠΡΒ

✝СΤΟΜΕΝ·
✝СΤΟΜΕΝ
✝СΤΟΜΕΝ
ΠΡΟСΧΟΜΕΝ
ΕΝΙΡΙΝΗΤω
ΕΛΕωС
ΘΥСΙΑ
ΗΑΓΑΠΙΤΥΘΥ
ΚΑΙΗΧΑΡΗС
ΚΑΙСΡΣΗΜωΝ
ΕΦΗΜΑС
ΑΔΡΙΑΝΟΥΠΑΤΡΙΑΡ
ΜΝΗСΘΗΤΙΚΕ
СΟΥΙωΑΝΝΟΥ
ΠΡΕСΒΥΤΕΡΟΥ
ΓΙΑСΑΓΑΘΗС

✝ΜΝΗСΘΗΤΙΚΕΤΥΛΛΥ
✝ΜΝ   ✝ΑΠ
ΚΕ·ΤΚΑ   ΘΗ
ΚΙΥ
ΜΕΗ
ΠΟΝ
ΑΔΡΙ
ΑΝΥ
Π+Β
ΙΑΡΧ

M10036

Plate VIIIb
Clementinus diptych (reverse). (Reduced)

begins – as in all eastern consular diptychs – on the R hand panel. We may note the Greek monogram and the new Christian element of the cross top centre. Clementinus' diptych is one of a series issued by eastern consuls who were members or adherents of the house of the emperor Anastasius (Cameron). Those surviving are: Areobindus (506), Clementinus (513), Anthemius (515), Anastasius (517) and Probus Magnus (518).[3] The main elements in common are: the consul's sceptre and stool, the supporting figures of Rome and Constantinople, the largesse at the consular games (Areobindus); sceptre, stool and imperial medallions (Anthemius and Anastasius); sceptre, stool, double footstool, Rome and Constantinople, largesse at the games (Probus Magnus). Like some other members of this connection (Cameron, 1978, p.272), Clementinus was a prominent monophysite, a religious position that defined political affiliation in the East for much of the 6th century.

Verso. The prayers are a good and early example of the reuse of a consular diptych in the Christian liturgy.[4] The panels would be set up on the altar so that the donor – here John, priest of St Agatha – would be remembered at the appropriate point in the Mass. The added text, on behalf of Pope Hadrian I, Andrew Machera and John the priest, dated 772, invokes the Virgin Mary (L panel) and St Agatha (R panel). It may well indicate a new set of donors and another church. The reference to Hadrian I, 'patriarch of the city', suggests that these donors lived in Rome. In that case, the likely (though not certain) recipient is the church of St Agatha *in Subura*, otherwise called St Agata dei Goti, in the centre of Rome, north-east of the forum of Trajan.[5] A Greek community may have been established there in the earlier 8th century.[6]

Provenance. In the collection of Joachim Negelein of Nürnberg (1675–1749) in the mid-18th century,[7] and the Wiczay collection in Hédervár at the end of the century. Thence to Fejérváry in 1834.

Gori, I.229–62 and pls ix–x; Pulszky 1844, Roman 4; Henszlmann 660; Pulszky 29–30; Waring, *Sculpture*, pl.I.2, p.7; Maskell, p.168; Westwood 54–5 ('58.4–5); Meyer 13; BFAC 26; Delbrueck 16, *LI* 13; *MRT* 100; Volbach 15; Alan Cameron, 'The house of Anastasius', *Greek Roman and Byzantine Studies* 19 (1978), pp.259–76, at p.274; *Age of Spirituality* 48; J.-M. Sansterre, 'Où le diptyche consulaire de Clementinus fut-il remployé à une fin liturgique?', *Byzantion* 54 (1984), pp.641–7, pls i–ii; Alan Cameron, 'A new late antique ivory: the Fauvel panel', *American Journal of Archaeology* 88 (1984), pp.397–402; R. Bagnall et al., *Consuls of the Later Roman Empire*, Philological Monographs of the American Philological Association 36 (Atlanta, Georgia, 1987), p.561.

1   *PLRE* ii.303, with references.

2   See the liturgies of St James and St John Chrysostom, at the anaphora, preceding the consecration: F.E. Brightman, *Liturgies Eastern and Western* (Oxford, 1896), pp.49 and 383. Our text adds: ΣΤΟΜΕΝ ΕΥΛΑΒΟΣ and Η ΑΓΑΠΙΤΟΥ . . . ΕΦ ΗΜΑΣ ΑΜΗΝ.

3   Volbach 8–24bis; see further *PLRE* ad loc. Areobindus, Anastasius and Probus Magnus are demonstrably related to the emperor Anastasius. Clementinus and Anthemius have the same style of diptych. Orestes (western consul 530), a relative of Probus Magnus, issued a diptych (Volbach 31) in the same style. It is thought to be a Clementinus diptych recut, with the consul's portrait and the imperial medallions altered: N. Netzer, 'Redating the consular ivory of Orestes', *Burlington Magazine* 125 (1983), pp.267–71, figs. 10–17; see further Cameron (1984).

4   A consular diptych of Justinian was inscribed with a neumed text in the 11th century, perhaps at Autun (Delbrueck 27); and two ivory tablets 'cum gradualibus' are recorded in an inventory of Bamberg cathedral in the earlier twelfth: B. Bischoff, *Mittelalterliche Schatzverzeichnisse* I, Veröffentlichungen des Zentralinstituts für Kunstgeschichte in München IV (Munich, 1967) 6, p.18, line 46.

5   R. Krautheimer et al., *Corpus Basilicarum Christianarum Romae* 5 vols (Vatican City, 1937–77), i.2–12. Other dedications to St Agatha within Rome are: St Agatha *caput Africae* (near S. Stefano Rotondo); St Agatha in Trastevere (not mentioned however in literary sources before the 12th century); an oratory 'in monasterio Tempuli' and St Agatha 'in diaconia'. See *Liber Pontificalis*, ed. L. Duchesne, 2 vols, Bibliothèque des Écoles françaises d'Athènes et de Rome, 2 ser.III (Paris, 1886–92), ii.24 and 12. For St Agatha *in Subura* see also the 'Einsiedeln Itinerary', routes 3, 5 and 7: R. Valentini and G. Zuchetti, *Codice Topografice della Città di Roma*, 2 vols (Rome, 1942), ii.185, 189, 192. An alternative provenance is St Agatha in Catania (Sicily), the centre of a flourishing cult in the 7th–8th century and an area in which Greek was spoken.

6   By Gregory II (715–31). But see H. Geertman, who considers that there is insufficient evidence either way: *More Veterum: Il 'Liber Pontificalis' e gli edifici ecclesiastici di Roma nella tarda antichità e nell' alto medioevo*, Archaeologica Traiectina 10 (Groningen, 1975), p.116, citing *Liber Pontificalis* i.402.

7   Joachim's son, Gustav Philip Negelein made the diptych the subject of his inaugural dissertation in the philosophy faculty at Altdorf: *Dissertatio inauguralis de uetusto quodam diptycho consulari et ecclesiastico* (Altdorf, 1742), extensively quoted by Gori.

2

Early Medieval

The tradition of ivory-carving that is so consummately expressed in Nos 5–8 persisted well into the 6th century. The proof lies in the throne of Maximian, bishop of Ravenna (546–56). This curved-back ivory chair (Volbach 140) was a model familiar to Carolingian artists, and remarkably survives largely intact today. Fifty years later this antique tradition had ceased: ivory was not available even in the Mediterranean, still less further north. Bone inlay continued (No.4c), at a relatively primitive level. Why this was so is not yet clear. Contributory factors no doubt were: (a) the Islamic conquest of North Africa;[1] (b) the disruption of trade-patterns with central or coastal Africa, and between the new Islamic world and the Byzantine Empire; and (c) changing fashions in patronage in barbarian Europe. But any of these obstacles could have been overcome; it remains a puzzle that ivory-carving ceased to be practised so suddenly and so universally.

The revival comes at the court of Charlemagne (771–814).[2] Late antique models were freely available; and the first generation of Carolingian artists emulated them with great skill. For example the Lorsch Gospels, splendid in themselves, had a luxury binding set with five-part panels back and front of Christ and the Virgin, each of which is at only one remove from an antique model.[3] The major Carolingian panel in Liverpool (No.9) belongs to the next generation: 814–40, the reign of Louis the Pious. Now with greater confidence artists are taking elements from the antique store and adapting them to the requirements of contemporary theology and devotion.

Ivory remains scarce. The 9th and 10th centuries are pre-eminently the era of planing down the verso of an antique diptych as the basis for carving, or even planing off the recto (No.9). Thus panels are thinner than in the days of plenty, and often fragile. The exception is the series of panels carved for the archbishop of Magdeburg, c.980, three of which are in Liverpool (Nos 11–13). Here the artists had plenty of good thick ivory to work on, such as was available in contemporary Byzantium, but not in the West. We may conjecture that it came via the Empress Theophanu and her entourage.

In the absence of elephant ivory, Northern Europe had two substitutes: walrus ivory, also called 'morse' (No.15) and whalebone (No.14). Walrus has a more restricted area that can be worked, and the carving is less sharply defined;[4] but it has a translucence of its own. Whalebone, more correctly 'baleen',[5] by contrast offers a working area comparable with elephant ivory, sharp definition, but a surface that is now rough and unattractive.

The 11th century saw ivory workshops in Liège under Bishop Notker, and in the Meuse region as a whole.[6] But ivory was still relatively hard to obtain, and thus perforce not a preferred medium for 11th-century luxury goods in Western Europe.

1 By the late 7th century the whole of Roman Africa was under Islamic control. Such ivory carving as continued was in a different tradition, though one which still borrowed elements from late Roman art: see E. Kühnel, *Die Islamischen Elfenbeinskulpturen VIII–XIII Jahrhundert* (Berlin, 1971). The crux is rather the changing trade-patterns with Byzantium and barbarian Europe. Here we have too little information even to speculate.

2 A few pieces of high-quality ivory-carving in a 'northern' style survive from the later 8th century, notably the Genoels-Eldern panels of Christ and the Virgin now in Brussels (Goldschmidt I.1–2). These had no stylistic influence on the revival at the court of Charlemagne – though some iconographic and technical influence may be conjectured.

3 Volbach 223–4.

4 The lack of definition in walrus ivory could be counteracted by gold and coloured paint. See P. Williamson and L. Webster, 'The coloured decoration of Anglo-Saxon ivory carvings', *Early Medieval Wall-Painting and Painted Sculpture in England*, ed. S. Cather, D. Park and P. Williamson, BAR British Series 216 (Oxford, 1990), pp.177–94.

5 MacGregor, p.21, with good drawings.

6 See for example the portable altar set with walrus ivory formerly in Melk, Austria (Goldschmidt I.105) now in Dumbarton Oaks (Weitzmann, no.34, pls lxii–lxvi), and for the subject as a whole J. Philippe, *Evangélaire de Notger et la chronologie de l'art mosan des époques pré-romane et romane* (Brussels, 1956).

9

Crucifixion with Women at the Sepulchre

*c.*820–840   Northern French

M 8022

Pls IXa–h

Ivory. 160 × 108 × 6 mm.

A later hole in the centre of the upper frame has caused the crack running *c.*90 mm. towards centre R; further damage in lower R frame. The image is raised proud of the acanthus frame and is markedly rubbed, as the frame is not. The verso is a recessed panel 154 × 96 mm., the outer frame surviving only in its lower L edge (Pl.IXd, L panel). It is thus possible that the piece is an older ivory reused, in which the recto may have been planed down for a new image. Two chisel-marks on each side of the verso, and crosses XXXX top to bottom at L and R, would secure the panel to a binding or other base. Marked in ink on the verso RC 1 (= Pulszky 1844). Traces of gilding on the angel.

Crucifixion, beneath *tabula ansata* inscribed IESVS NAZAREN' / REX IVDAEORVM; busts of the sun (L) and moon (R) in the heaven above. Christ wears a knee-length *perizonium* tied at the centre.[1] Below him (L) Longinus, with spear in his L hand, gestures with his R hand to acknowledge 'Certainly this was a righteous man' (Luke 23:47). Below Christ (R) Stephaton, with *situla* to L at his feet, fixes the vinegar-filled sponge to a reed (John 19:29). Far L the Virgin weeps; far R St John the Evangelist holds his gospelbook in his L hand. In the lower scene is a Roman tomb: it is built in brick, with a cornice below the dome; the arched cupola has a double finial on top. Two sleeping soldiers – the one in front with spear and shield – fail to guard Christ's sepulchre (Matthew 27:62–28:7). The stone that blocked the entry provides a seat for an angel, with a staff in his L hand, who raises his R hand to address the three women approaching from R. The fine acanthus frame is delimited on the inside and outside by a plain strip (1 mm. wide), which is double, except to the L of the sepulchre. The Virgin's R hand, the L wall of the sepulchre and the front soldier's spear encroach on the frame to the L and (base of the spear) below.

This ivory reflects two classical models. The *tabula ansata* and the sun and moon have been taken over from Late Antique official art.[2] More remarkably the lower scene depends on the early 5th-century Ascension with the Women at the Sepulchre that is now in Munich (Pl.IXb).[3] The sepulchre here has the statue of a philosopher to the R of the doors, and a second statue implied to the L; the (closed) doors are shown more distinctly. Both soldiers are behind the tomb, and the angel, here wearing sandals, has no staff. The women approach with virtually the same gestures in the same order. There can be no serious doubt that the Carolingian artist had seen and studied this antique model. But whereas the original shows the risen Christ climbing up to grasp the hand of God in heaven, the Carolingian derivative is in three sections: heaven, delimited by the clouds below sun and moon and the horizontal bar of the Cross; the Crucifixion, delimited by a thick, wavy piece of ground – a device well-known in the Utrecht psalter, *c.*820;[4] and the Sepulchre scene below, in which moving the angel to the R has brought the sepulchre to the lower edge, out of the way of the Crucifixion scene.

In Late Antiquity the Crucifixion was shown as a rapid sketch in a narrative sequence, as for example in the wooden doors of S. Sabina in Rome, *c.*432.[5] By the 8th century, however, it could be presented as a subject for meditation.[6] The Liverpool ivory is in this more recent tradition, inviting the viewer to pause and identify with each of the four figures beneath the Cross: the distraught Virgin, the enlightened Longinus, the merciful Stephaton, and St John – the witness, carrying his gospelbook. The theologians at the court of Charlemagne may have had some difficulty with this presentation, in that they were steering a careful path between Byzantine iconoclasm and what their Greek critics might term idolatrous representation of holy persons.[7] But by the 820s there was less anxiety on this latter count, Western theology was developing on its own; and the Crucifixion remained a central image.

Plate IXa
Crucifixion with Women at the Sepulchre

In modern scholarship the Liverpool ivory raises the contentious issue of duplicates, or near-duplicates, in Carolingian art. These are rare, though not unknown: there is a striking instance of two panels of the Wedding at Cana.[8] The formula of the Liverpool ivory is closely matched in a panel now in Honolulu (Pl.IXd and f),[9] and more remotely copied in the later and less skilful panel that is now in Baltimore (Pl.IXh).[10] The Honolulu panel is also related to a panel of the Ascension, formerly in Berlin (Pl.IXg).[11] Taken together, these two pairs (the Wedding at Cana and the Crucifixion) encourage us to regard ivories as we do manuscript illumination: as a medium in which legitimate, contemporary duplication did take place – though not of course on the scale required of consular diptychs.

Provenance. Bought by Fejérváry by 1844 from J.D. Böhm, Vienna.

Pulszky 1844, Christian Roman 1; Henszlmann 681; Pulszky 36; Waring, p.9 (drawing); Maskell, p.169; Westwood 239 ('55.14); Gatty 29; Graeven i.1; Goldschmidt I.139; BFAC 40; *LI* 16; *MRT* 101; Volbach 229; Gaborit-Chopin, pl.61.

Plate IXb
Ascension with Women at the Sepulchre.
Bayerisches Nationalmuseum, Munich

1   In manuscript illumination the older type of *perizonium* (early 9th century) is knotted in the middle, as here; the newer type (*c*.820+) is knotted at the side: Mütherich, pp.38–9; see also R. Haussherr, *Der tote Christus am Kreuz: zur Ikonographie des Gerokreuzes* (Bonn, 1963), pp.108–11 and 122.

2   For the *tabula ansata* see Nos 5–6 and 8 above; and for the sun and moon replacing the imperial portraits (cf. No.8, note 3) see Volbach 137.

3   Munich, Bayerisches Nationalmuseum MA 157: Volbach 110. Christ's halo is a later addition.

4   Utrecht, Rijksuniversiteit, MS 32, a manuscript written and illustrated for Archbishop Ebbo of Rheims (816–47): facsimile ed. K. van der Horst and J.H.A. Engelbregt, *Utrecht-Psalter*, Codices Selecti 75 (Graz, 1984).

5   G. Jeremias, *Die Holztür der Basilika S. Sabina in Rom*, Bilderhefte des deutschen archäologischen Instituts Rom 7 (Tübingen, 1980), pp.60–3, pl.52. Another good example is London, British Museum MLA 56.6–23.5: Volbach 116.

6   See the frescoes of the first half of the 8th century in S. Maria Antiqua, Rome: P. Romanelli and P.J. Nordhagen, *S. Maria Antiqua* (Rome, 1964), pls.22–8 (Pope John VII) and pl.vii (Pope Zacharias).

7   The court position is set out in detail in the *Libri Carolini*: ed. H. Bastgen in Monumenta Germaniae Historica, *Leges* III, *Concilia* II, Supplement (Hanover, 1924).

8   A. von Euw, 'Elfenbeinarbeiten des 9. bis 12. Jahrhunderts', in *Rhein und Maas: Kunst und Kultur 800–1400*, 2 vols (Cologne, 1973), ii.377–86, showing Goldschmidt I.46 and 47.

9   Honolulu Academy of Arts 672.1 (acquired 1948); first recorded 1888 in the collection of Friedrich Schneider, canon of Mainz. See further A. Goldschmidt, in *Mitteilungen des Museum-Verbandes*, March 1933, no.691, pp.6–7. In October 1983 the two panels were studied together in a seminar in the Victoria & Albert Museum.

10   Walters Art Gallery, Baltimore 71.142: see Randall 245 and colorplate 65, dated 870–80.

11   Goldschmidt I.140, a panel that was in St Maximin, Trier from at least the 13th century: H.W. Kuhn, 'Das politische Programm des Liber aureus von St. Maximin (Trier): Untersuchungen über Chartular und Prachteinband aus dem 13. Jahrhundert', *Jahrbuch für westdeutsche Landesgeschichte* 4 (1978), pp.81–128 at pp.113–28 and pls.2–3 (Pl.IXg). It is one of the ivories (no.32) from the Kaiser-Friedrich-Museum, Berlin which was very badly damaged in 1945. Compared with the Honolulu panel, it had the same acanthus border (a fragment of which survives) and virtually the same dimensions (146 × 105 mm. Berlin; 148 × 104 mm. Honolulu).

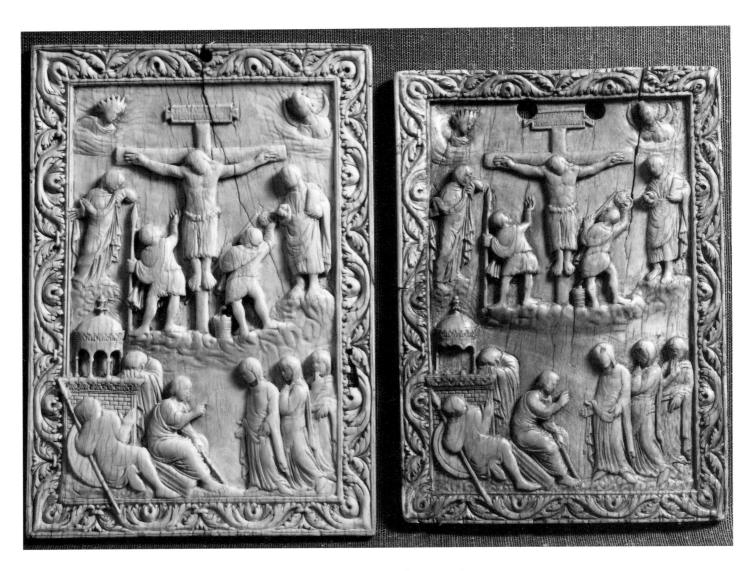

Plate IXc–d
(Left) *The Liverpool Crucifixion with Women at the Sepulchre and* (right) *the Honolulu Crucifixion with Women at the Sepulchre* (obverse). Photograph courtesy of the Board of Trustees of the Victoria & Albert Museum, London

Plate IXe–f
(Left) *The Liverpool Crucifixion with Women at the Sepulchre and* (right) *the Honolulu Crucifixion with Women at the Sepulchre* (reverse). Photograph courtesy of the Board of Trustees of the Victoria & Albert Museum, London

Plate IXg
The Berlin Ascension. Staatliche Museen zu Berlin

Plate IXh
The Baltimore Crucifixion with Women at the Sepulchre.
Walters Art Gallery, Baltimore

Plate Xa
Ascension

10

Ascension

9th century   Northern French

M 8021

Pls Xa–c

Ivory. 93 × 61 × 5 mm.

Two later holes at centre and R of the bottom margin. Slight cracks in the outer margins, but general condition excellent. Cataloguers' notes: on the R edge 6; on the back RC 2 (=Pulszky 1844), 209, BB (or 33), X.

Christ ascends to heaven in the presence of six disciples, who show varying human reactions: the two outer figures L and R, each holding a scroll, are dazzled; the central figures alarmed (L) and unwilling to let Christ go (R). Compared with the Late Antique Ascension (Pl.IXb), the tree still gives a sense of height; but Christ has lost touch with the ground, his sandals and scroll are gone, and the additional cloak in his R hand only prevents his grasping the Hand of God. His posture is a compromise between looking towards heaven and turning back to the onlookers below.[1] The image is deeply sunk in a plain acanthus frame with a narrow inner strip and a slightly wider outer edge.

The artist here was still in touch with a Late Antique model.[2] It is a single scene in which the onlookers respond directly to the departing Christ, rather than a two-tier presentation (Pl.IXg), with interpreting angels, eleven disciples and the Virgin herself. Other Carolingian Ascension ivories all to some degree verge towards this doctrinal statement of the divinity of Christ, rather than the record of a historical event.[3] In the Liverpool panel Christ has neither halo nor cross nor mandorla. The panel has long been associated with two others of the same size in virtually identical acanthus frames: the Annunciation, and the Women at the Sepulchre (Pls Xb–c).[4] Differences in the disposition of the scenes and in the figure-drawing are attributed to the exemplars from which the artist(s) worked. But it may be questioned whether the very routine acanthus frame is sufficient to link these three panels with any security.[5]

Plate Xb
Annunciation. Staatliche Museen zu Berlin

Plate Xc
Women at the Sepulchre. Courtesy of the Board of Trustees of the Victoria & Albert Museum, London

Provenance. Fejérváry had acquired it by 1844.

Pulszky 1844, Christian Roman 2; Henszlmann 665; Pulszky 37; Westwood 244 ('58.10); Gatty 30; Maskell, pp.139, 169; Graeven i.2; Nelson I, no.I; Goldschmidt I.127; BFAC 39; S. Gutberlet, *Die Himmelfahrt Christi in der bildenden Kunst* (Strasbourg, 1934); *LI* 17; *MRT* 102.

---

1   See Gutberlet, pp.172–3, pl.X and A.A. Schmid, 'Himmelfahrt Christi', in *Lexikon der christlichen Ikonographie*, 8 vols (Rome, etc., 1968–76), ii.268–76.

2   See further G. Jeremias, *Die Holztür der Basilika S. Sabina in Rom*, Bilderhefte des deutschen archäologischen Instituts Rom 7 (Tübingen, 1980), pp.68–76, and pls. 60–5.

3   The classic statement of the doctrinal Ascension is in the Rabbula Gospels of 586: K. Weitzmann, *Late Antique and Early Christian Book Illumination* (London, 1977), p.101 and pl.36 (fol.13v). Christ is top centre, facing the onlooker. He is nimbed, in a mandorla and supported by angels. Below stands the Virgin *orans*, with two angels instructing the Apostles. It is a forceful statement of orthodoxy against the Arians. Of the 19 Carolingian Ascension

ivories listed by Goldschmidt, all but the Liverpool panel exhibit some of these doctrinal features. Add a 20th, with the same doctrinal characteristics, London, British Museum, MLA 78.3–1.1: see D. Buckton, 'A Carolingian Ascension ivory', British Museum Occasional Papers 10 (London, 1980), pp.17–20 and pl.1.

4   Goldschmidt I.125, Berlin Kaiser-Friedrich-Museum 5932 (92 × 61 mm.); and Goldschmidt I.126, London, Victoria & Albert Museum 380.1871 (93 × 60 mm.): see Pls Xb–c. The Berlin panel was destroyed in 1945.

5   The three panels (Goldschmidt I.125–7) are briefly considered by U. Surmann, *Studien zur ottonischen Elfenbeinplastik in Metz und Trier*, Beiträge zur Kunstgeschichte 5 (Bonn, 1990), pp.9–10, who thinks it likely that they were cut in Fulda.

11–13
Magdeburg panels

*c.*980   ?Trier

M 8061, M 8062, M 8017

Pls XI–XIII, XIIIa–c

Three panels from the so-called 'Magdeburg antependium': one from the Fejérváry collection (M 8017), the other two acquired independently by Joseph Mayer (M 8061 and M 8062).

11
Christ commissioning the Apostles
(Luke 9:2)[1]

M 8061

Pl.XI

Ivory. 129 × 118 × 8 mm.; margin 18–20 mm.

Later holes at the four corners, with traces of metal washers, especially top R. Cracks down centre and top L, where a small piece of the *à jour* carving has been dislodged and glued back into place. Otherwise a sturdy piece in good condition. Nothing inscribed or written on the verso.

Christ with a nimbed halo, barefoot, with a scroll in his L hand, addresses twelve disciples, of whom only the leader, bearded, tonsured and also barefoot, is shown in full profile. The eyes of Christ and the leading disciple are drilled. The background *à jour* crosses with single incised borders, and the whole image sunk within the broad, plain outer frame.

Provenance. Magdeburg, *c.*980; Hallesches Heiltum *c.*1520; Possenti collection, Fabriano *c.*1820; Joseph Mayer by 1855.
Guardbook 42b; Maskell, p.170; Gatty 42; Graeven i.3; Nelson I, no.III; Goldschmidt II.8 (giving Possenti provenance); BFAC 41; *LI* 18; *MRT* 103.

12
Peter finds the Tribute-money
(Matthew 17:27)

M 8062

Pl.XII

Ivory. 129 × 118 × 8 mm.; margin 18–19 mm.

Later holes at the four corners, with traces of metal washers, as No.11. Nothing inscribed or written on the verso. Condition excellent.

Christ, with a nimbed halo, barefoot, with a scroll in his L hand, touches St Peter on the shoulder. Peter breaks open the jaws of the fish that he has just caught with rod and line, and removes the coin from its mouth. Seven disciples look on, the leader pressing on Christ, and two others being shown half-profile (L) and head-on (R). All five leading figures have drilled eyes. The background *à jour* squares with bevelled corners, forming a pattern of crosses slightly taller than they are broad.

Provenance. Magdeburg, *c.*980; Hallesches Heiltum *c.*1520; Possenti collection, Fabriano *c.*1820; Joseph Mayer by 1855.
Guardbook 42a; Waring, p.11 (drawing); Maskell, p.171; Gatty 41; Graeven i.3; Nelson I, no.II; Goldschmidt II.11 (giving Possenti provenance); BFAC 42; *LI* 19; *MRT* 103.

13
Christ and the Adulteress
(John 8:2–11)

M 8017

Pl.XIII

Ivory. 110 × 102 × 6–7 mm.; margin 7 mm.

Outer frame cut down to 7 mm., and the whole surface quite seriously rubbed. Nothing inscribed or written on the verso.

Christ, with a nimbed halo, barefoot, seated on a folding stool against the wall, bends down to write on a footstool on the ground in the atrium of the Temple (John 8:2). Two bas-relief heads on the footstool.[2] Four supporting disciples above L; and from the R the Adulteress and four of her accusers. The eyes of Christ and the other five main figures are drilled. An architectural setting with simplified acanthus

Plate XI
Christ commissioning the Apostles

Plate XII
Peter finds the Tribute-money

Plate XIII
Christ and the Adulteress

Plate XIIIa
Casket with ivory panels in the Hallesches Heiltum.
Hofbibliothek, Aschaffenburg

capitals on each column and beading round the arch; the *à jour* carving limited to the three windows and the door of the Temple. The vertical line top quasi-centre helps to create the illusion that the windows and door are centred, rather than pushed to the R to accommodate Christ's halo and L hand.

Provenance. Magdeburg *c.*980; Fejérváry from Böhm by 1844.

Pulszky 1844, Medieval 2; Henszlmann 669; Pulskzy 41; Waring, p.11 (drawing); Maskell, p.170; Westwood 312 ('54.60); Gatty 40; Graeven i.2; Goldschmidt II.13; BFAC 43; *LI* 20; *MRT* 103.

All three panels (Nos 11–13) belong to the series made *c.*980 for the archbishop of Magdeburg.[3] Sixteen survive, and two others are known from an early 16th-century drawing.[4] They may originally have constituted, or adorned, an altar-frontal – hence the convenient term 'Magdeburg antependium' – or an archiepiscopal throne; but already by the mid-11th century they were being detached and reused. Four were set in the front cover of the *Codex Wittekindeus*, now in Berlin;[5] and eventually another eight, including No.11 and arguably No.12, were set in a reliquary made for Archbishop Albrecht's treasury of relics at Halle *c.*1520 (Pl.XIIIa).[6] No.11 is on the extreme R of the front. That No.12 is one of the four panels on the back may be argued from the four attachment holes, which match both those in No.11 and those in the three other candidates for the back of the reliquary: Goldschmidt II.5 (Darmstadt), II.6 (London, British Museum: Pl.XIIIc) and II.9 (Paris, Louvre). The key 'donor' panel, showing Otto I presenting Magdeburg cathedral to Christ

(Pl.XIIIb) is now in New York. Whereas the ultimate Magdeburg provenance is clear, the date is in dispute, as is the location of the workshop where the panels were made. I have become convinced that they make better sense as Otto II's commemoration of his father's work than as Otto I's own gift to Magdeburg cathedral when the archbishopric was established in 968.[7] I share too Peter Lasko's sense that they were made north of the Alps:[8] to me the historical and social evidence indicates that S. Maximin, Trier is the most feasible and likely source of artists.

Nos 11 and 12, and very probably No.13, are by the same artist. In No.13 the single edge to the cross in Christ's halo is a minor difference, and the more solid treatment of the *à jour* carving is explicable: the artist must show the Temple. Judging by his 'tonsured' hair, Peter appears in all three.[9] No.12 has a curiously Late Antique section of sea, bottom R. No.13 shows the shoes and leggings that are normally worn by those in the world (the shod: as distinct from Christ and his disciples) in the other panels. No.11 is a static instant; in Nos 12–13 the action moves to and fro. In No.12 the eye is

Plate XIIIb
Otto I presents Magdeburg cathedral to Christ.
The Metropolitan Museum of Art, New York

Plate XIIIc
(Left) *Byzantine Vision of Ezekiel and* (right) *Widow of Nain.* Trustees of the British Museum, London

drawn to the R, from Christ's initial command to Peter's catching the fish, discovering the coin and then (to L) reporting back to Christ. No.13 is a dialogue, first between Christ and the leading accuser (John 8:4–8), with his hand in the Adulteress' sleeve; then between Christ and the Adulteress (John 8:10–11). 'Hath no man condemned thee?'; 'No man, Lord'.

Iconographically Nos 11–13 are very hard to match in earlier Western art. In the series as a whole there are points of contact with the wall-paintings of Abbot Witkowo (985–97) in Reichenau,[10] and with the *Codex Egberti* that was presented by two Reichenau men 977 / 93 to the archbishop of Trier.[11] The elongated fingers showing initiative and response are familiar in the contemporary manuscript illumination of Reichenau itself and its northern contacts in Cologne and Trier. But none of this adds up to solid sources. On the one hand the Magdeburg panels are an early and astonishingly extensive example of the New Testament cycle as developed in Ottonian art. On the other the panels have a background in Byzantium. The ivory itself is cut to a thickness and dimensions that can be paralleled only in a few contemporary Byzantine panels, such as the Vision of Ezekiel in the British Museum (Pl.XIIIc). It too was surely one of a series. Compared with another Magdeburg panel, the Widow of Nain, that is conveniently also in the British Museum (Pl.XIIIc) the Byzantine piece is taller, even thicker, and technically more sophisticated in its layers of carving.[12] Nevertheless one can visualise a Magdeburg artist finding in such a panel broad practical guidelines for his own work. Nos 11–13 are at the interface of Ottonian and Byzantine art – just as Nos 9–10 throw light on the relation of Late Antique art to Carolingian.

---

1 Probably Luke 9:1–6, within the context of Christ's teaching and miracles, rather than his final injunction just before the Ascension (Matthew 28:18–20).

2 Christ wrote twice on the ground (John 8:6 and 8), but what he wrote is not recorded. The Hitda Codex (Cologne, *c.*1020: fol.171) has 'TERRA TERRAM ACCUSAT'. Much later, *c.*1160, Peter Comestor, commenting John 8, cites two letters of St Ambrose, quoting respectively 'Terra, terra, absorbe hos uiros abdicatos' and 'Terra terram accusat': *Epp.*VII.50.4, to Studio and cf.IX.68.13–14, to Irenaeus (ed. M. Zelzer, *Sancti Ambrosii Opera* X.ii, CSEL 82 (Vienna, 1990), pp.57–8 and 174–5). The former refers to the earth swallowing Dathan and Abiram (Numbers 16:1–35, at 29–32): *Historia Scholastica* 98 (Migne, *PL* 198.1587A, with two essential corrections from MS Oxford, Bodleian Library, Bodley 164, fol. 177rb: Ambrose for Jerome, and *absorbe* for *scribe.*). Such a cross-reference, which was probably accessible to Ottonian exegetes, would explain the two heads.

3 Goldschmidt II.4–16; III.301–3. See now P. Lasko, *Ars Sacra* (Harmondsworth, 1972), pp.87–91; C.T. Little, 'From Milan to Magdeburg: the place of the Magdeburg ivories in Ottonian art', *Atti del 10° Congresso internazionale di studi sull' alto medioevo, Milan 26–30 settembre 1983* (Spoleto, 1986), pp.441–51; and M. Gibson, *The Magdeburg ivories in their social context*, Kresge Art Museum Occasional Papers 1 (East Lansing, 1994).

4 Pl.XIIIa: see note 6 below. The two lost panels there illustrated are the first and second to the L: the Wedding at Cana and Christ healing the Blind Man.

5 Berlin, Deutsche Staatsbibliothek, MS Theol.Lat.fol.1: see V. Rose, *Verzeichniss der lateinischen Handschriften der Königlichen Bibliothek zu Berlin* II.i (Berlin, 1901), 265, pp.42–3.

6 Known now principally from a contemporary pilgrims' guide illustrated with excellent drawings: facsimile by P.M. Halm and R. Berliner, *Das Hallesche Heiltum* (Berlin, 1931). The entry relevant to the Magdeburg panels is no.VIII.6 (pp.58–9 and pl.153 = our Pl.XIIIa): 'Eyn Silbernn vbergulte Sarch mit viij Elffenbeynen teffeleyn. Doreyn Acht historien ausz den Evangelien geschnitten . . . ' (Aschaffenburg, Hofbibliothek, MS 14, fol.355v–56).

7 Gibson, 1994 (note 3 above).

8 Lasko, *op.cit.* (note 3 above), p.91.

9 Peter's hair-style had been established since the 6th century: see for example the mosaics in San Vitale, Ravenna and in SS Cosmas and Damian, Rome.

10 K. Martin, *Die ottonischen Wandbilder der St. Georgskirche Reichenau-Oberzell* (Sigmaringen, 1975), pls.6, 11 and 13. See also C.R. Dodwell, *Painting in Europe 800–1200* (Harmondsworth, 1971), pp.49–51 and pl.52.

11 H. Mayr-Harting, *Ottonian Book-Illumination*, 2 vols (London, 1991), ii.70–81, pls V–VII, with references. See also conveniently G. Franz and F.J. Ronig, *Codex Egberti der Stadtbibliothek Trier: Entstehung und Geschichte der Handschrift* (Wiesbaden, 1984).

12 The Ezekiel panel is London, British Museum, MLA 56.5–9.1 (Goldschmidt-Weitzmann II.16), later 10th century, measuring 151 × 121 × 10 mm. The Widow of Nain panel is London, British Museum, MLA 56.6–23.25 (Goldschmidt II.6), measuring 124 × 118 × 8 mm. (much as Nos 11–13). The inner frame of the Byzantine panel is canted at *c.*.60°; the inner frame of the Magdeburg panel is a straight right angle. Again the Byzantine panel is carved in several layers (e.g. the angels, top R, and the footstool, bottom R), whereas all the Magdeburg panels are carved in a single layer.

Plate XIVa
Baldricus panel. (Reduced)

14

Baldricus

10th–11th century   ?Liège

M 10037

Pls XIVa–c

Whalebone. 355 × 130 × 5.5 mm.

A single panel of whalebone, with a small crack bottom R and the brown, pitted surface that seems to be characteristic of medieval whalebone; otherwise in good condition. On the verso two nails upper R edge, and two holes lower R edge. Verso top, three lines in ink, 19th century, not now legible, ending 'Baldricus'.

Apart from the inscription at the top, PIO PRAESVLE / BALDRICO IVBENTE ('by the devout command of Bishop Baldric'), the panel derives from the consular diptych of Probus Magnus. We have already seen (No.8) that this diptych itself belongs to a sequence running from Areobindus (506) to Probus Magnus (518). Two examples survive of the original Probus Magnus diptych: one in Paris (Pl.XIVb), the other in Milan.[1] Each now lacks both the identifying *tabula ansata* above and the scene of largesse at the games below. The Paris panel however is matched by a whalebone copy (also in Paris), which preserves the original inscription:

Fl[auius] Anastasius Paulus Probus /
Moschianus Probus Magnus (Pl.XIVc)[2]

Valuable though it is in preserving the text, this Paris whalebone panel is of very uncertain date; it could well be more recent than BALDRICVS. A plausible reconstruction would be that the Paris ivory (Pl.XIVb), in its complete state, was the model for both BALDRICVS and the Paris whalebone, thus:[3]

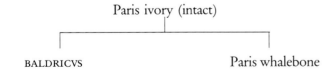

So far as in him lay, the carver of the Baldricus panel has made an exact copy of the central and lower sections of one panel of a consular diptych. Details of the consul's hairstyle, garments, shoes and ceremonial chair are all preserved, as are Rome and Constantinople, the hanging garland above and the largesse below.[4] There is no thought of adapting or Christianising the image; rather *praesul Baldricus* is presented

Plate XIVb
Probus Magnus panel, AD 518. Bibliothèque Nationale, Paris
(Cabinet des Médailles)

as a consul – as accurately as possible. Such a conceit belongs to the literary and political milieu of Otto III (983–1002) and the imperial court in the first half of the 11th century. The *renovatio Romani imperii*, the renewal or rebirth of the Roman empire, was a fundamental political assumption for virtually a century until the dispute over investiture (*c.*1075+)

fatally divided the interests of empire and papacy. So it was reasonable for a bishop to be a consul, a leading official in the new Roman polity.[5]

Such considerations may indicate which of the several bishops Baldric in the later 10th and 11th centuries is most likely to be our man. Baldric, bishop of Speyer (970–87) predates the great era of Speyer as an imperial centre, and seems to have made little impact on Ottonian government.[6] Baldric, archbishop of Utrecht (918–77) is of an older generation, for whom the *renovatio Romani imperii* might not translate immediately into the revival of consular diptychs. To my mind the leading candidate is Baldric II, bishop of Liège (1008–18): the topos of *renovatio* was by then familiar, Bishop Notker (969–1008) had established Liège as a major city in the Empire, and – not least – this is a great era of book-production in Liège and the Meuse valley. Notker himself commissioned at least one luxury binding, set with an autobiographical ivory panel.[7] As his successor, Baldric II continued his cultural initiative. The inscription, 'pio praesule Baldrico iubente' is a rhythmic Sapphic (Raby i.302). It would fit easily into the milieu of Liège in the first quarter of the 11th century.

Provenance. Fejérváry from Löwen in Cologne in 1836.[8]

Pulszky 1844, Roman 5; Henszlmann 662; Pulszky 32; Maskell, p.168; Westwood 63 ('54.87'); Meyer 19; A. Maskell, *Ivories* (London, 1905), pl.viii.6; BFAC 27; Delbrueck 25, considering the panel a 19th-century forgery; *LI* 14; F.J.E. Raby, *A History of Secular Latin Poetry in the Middle Ages*, 2 vols, 2 edn (Oxford, 1957); Volbach 24bis; A. Cameron, 'A new late antique ivory: the Fauvel panel', *American Journal of Archaeology* 88 (1984), pp.397–402 and pls 55–6; *Byzance* 16 (Probus Magnus 518).

Plate XIVc
Whalebone Probus Magnus panel. Bibliothèque Nationale, Paris (Cabinet des Médailles)

1 Paris, Bibliothèque Nationale, Cabinet des Médailles, no. 3267 (Pl.XIVb); and Milan, Castello Sforzesco, Ivories 31: Volbach 24 and 23 respectively.

2 Paris, Bibliothèque Nationale, Cabinet des Médailles, no. 3265 (Pl.XIVc): Volbach 24bis. For Volbach's opening 'H' read 'Fl'. For Probus Magnus see R.S. Bagnall et al., *Consuls of the Later Roman Empire*, Philological Monographs of the American Philological Association 36 (Atlanta, Georgia, 1987), p.571.

3 There is a clear parallel to the BALDRICVS panel in another whalebone panel, now in St Petersburg (Volbach 24bis), which is also a version of the Probus Magnus diptych. It is inscribed ARACONTI DEO VOTA ('Aracontus [offers his] prayers to God'); *pace* Volbach, not ARABONTI. But its date and context have yet to be clarified.

4 For the largesse cf. also No.8 (Pl.VIIIa) above. Note the crosses on the five silver dishes.

5 A vivid piece of literary evidence is Peter Damian's hymn to St Apollinaris: 'Consul aeterni trabeate regni', written for good measure in a quasi-Horatian Sapphic metre. Migne, PL 145. col. 951B.

6 Fleckenstein's classic analysis of episcopal participation in Carolingian and Ottonian politics features several 10th-century bishops of Speyer, but not Baldric himself: J. Fleckenstein, *Die Hofkapelle der deutschen Könige*, 2 vols, Schriften der Monumenta Germaniae Historica 16 (Stuttgart, 1959–66).

7 Goldschmidt II.44–6; see further *Rhein und Maas: Kunst und Kultur 800–1400*, 2 vols (Cologne, 1973), i.220–6, and J. Philippe, *L'évangelaire de Notger et la chronologie de l'art mosan des époques pré-romane et romane* (Brussels, 1956). I am unconvinced by the redating of this panel to the early 12th century: see P. Lasko, *Ars Sacra: 800–1200* (Harmondsworth, 1972), pp.163–5.

8 Pulszky 1844 *ad loc.* Caronni appears to refer to the existence of the Baldricus panel in Cologne in the Hupsch collection in 1806: 'e un' altra più piccola (oltra all' edita del Bianconi) che scoprii a Colonia presso del Medico Hupsch' (<F. Caronni> Barnabita, *Ragguaglio di alcuni monumenti di antiquità ed arti* (Milan, 1806), p.208).

15

Nativity

Late 10th century   English

M 8060

Pls XVa–d

Walrus ivory. 78 × 62 × 3–5 mm.

The panel is damaged top L and bottom R. The upper and lower borders have been cut down, and the R border may have been trimmed. The eyes of the three adult figures and the two animals are drilled and set with black glass.[1] A later hole upper centre. The verso shows clearly the striation of a cross-section of walrus ivory. Ink note, 'The Nativity', probably by W.H. Rolfe.

The Virgin lies on a wooden bed, her turbanned head supported on a pillow held by the midwife. Her R hand, on the edge of the bed, gestures down to the Child below. The finely-rendered folds of the sheet draw attention to the curious perspective of the bed itself, a problem which is not alleviated by the additional leg to the R of the animals. (The lower part of the leg at bottom R has been broken off.) Joseph sits on a stool with a cushion top R. The swaddled Child in the crib below, set in apparently rocky ground, is adored by ox (L) and ass (R).

English walrus ivory carving of the late 10th and early 11th centuries has traditionally been assigned *en bloc* to Winchester, being part of the cultural renaissance associated with Dunstan and Aethelwold.[2] The Liverpool panel has a close parallel in a miniature in the Benedictional of St Aethelwold (*c.*970: Pl.XVb).[3] In that several features of the ivory can only with severe difficulty be derived from the miniature,[4] the two may be seen as cousins, both dependent on an older model. A Carolingian casket now in Brunswick includes a strikingly apposite Nativity scene (Pl.XVc); and another such casket

Plate XVa
Nativity

now in the Louvre shows the sequence of Infancy scenes to which a Nativity panel might belong (Pl.XVd).[5] The Brunswick and Louvre caskets represent the sculptural tradition with which (along with Carolingian manuscripts) Dunstan became familiar as a wealthy exile in Ghent in 956–7.

Provenance. Excavated in or near Sandwich (Kent) by W.H. Rolfe; acquired by Joseph Mayer in 1858.

Publications of the Antiquarian Etching Club (London, 1854), V, p.vii and pl.32; Maskell, p.171; Gatty 43; Graeven i.7; Nelson I, No.IV; BFAC 73; Longhurst XIII; Goldschmidt IV.6; *LI* 27; *Ivory Carvings in Early Medieval England 700–1200*, Victoria & Albert Museum exhibition (London, 1974), 21; Beckwith 26; *MRT* 108; *The Golden Age of Anglo-Saxon Art 966–1066*, British Museum / British Library (London, 1984), 115; D.M. Wilson, *Anglo-Saxon Art from the seventh century to the Norman Conquest* (London, 1984), pp.190 and 192 (plate).

---

1   See P. Williamson and L. Webster, 'The coloured decoration of Anglo-Saxon ivory carvings', in *Early Medieval Wall Painting and Painted Sculpture in England*, ed. S. Cather, D. Park and P. Williamson, BAR, British Series 216 (Oxford, 1990), pp.177–94, at p.184.

2   Beckwith 26 and cf. pp.48–9.

3   London, British Library, MS Add.49598, fol.15v: facsimile by G.F. Warner and H.A. Wilson, *The Benedictional of St Aethelwold, bishop of Winchester 963–984*, The Roxburghe Club (London, 1910). See further R. Deshman, 'The iconography of the full-page miniatures of the Benedictional of Aethelwold', unpublished PhD (Princeton, 1970), p.22, fig.39; E. Temple, *Anglo-Saxon Manuscripts 900–1066*, A Survey of Manuscripts illuminated in the British Isles 2

(London, 1976), 23; R. Gameson, 'Manuscript art at Christ Church, Canterbury, in the generation after St Dunstan', in *St Dunstan: his life, times and cult*, ed. N. Ramsay, M. Sparks and T. Tatton-Brown (Woodbridge, 1992), pp.187–220, at p.210. The iconographic tradition continues in the Missal of Robert of Jumièges, Rouen, Bibliothèque Municipale, 274 (Y6), fol.32ᵛ: *Golden Age* 50, proposing a date of ? pre-1023.

4   Note in the ivory the Virgin's turban, Joseph's bare L leg, the Child's position within the crib, the extra leg to the bed, the absence of haloes.

5   Brunswick, Herzog Anton Ulrich-Museum MA 59 (Goldschmidt I.96) and Paris, Musée du Louvre, Objets d'art MRR 75 (Goldschmidt I.95).

Plate XVb
Benedictional of St Aethelwold. By permission of the British Library, London

Plate XVc
Brunswick casket. Herzog Anton Ulrich-Museum, Brunswick

Plate XVd
Louvre casket. Musée du Louvre, Paris

3

Byzantine

The development of Byzantine art was arrested, or redirected, by the emperor Leo III, who issued his edict against icons in 726. 'Iconoclasm' continued as a law – or a threat – until 843; and the recovery of Byzantine art, in Byzantium,[1] seems to have been delayed until the reign of Constantine Porphyrogenitus (*ob*.959). 'Middle Byzantine' ivories (Nos 16–21) may be dated *c*.950–*c*.1200: specifically the fall of Constantinople to the Crusading army in 1204. Within the broad span of the mid-10th century to the later 11th the fundamental work of Goldschmidt and Weitzmann has established five stylistic groups, with sub-groups appertaining.[2] This material can rarely be dated internally, even when an emperor is named; for the imperial names recur over the decades. The only secure dates are numismatic: certain Byzantine coins appear to date specific ivories. On this basis Ioli Kalavrezou-Maxeiner has argued that the 'Romanos' group of ivories (No.20) belongs to the later 11th century rather than the later 10th.[3] Her argument would reorder the traditional grouping quite radically: if the 'Triptych' group (Nos 17–19) is really dependent on 'Romanos', then it too loses a century of its age. These are matters for professional Byzantinists. At this point in the *Catalogue* (and here only) I have gone carefully, leaving all the Byzantine ivories with an open date of 10th–11th century. As to the location of the workshops, it is still a commonplace that sound iconography and technical competence were to be found in Constantinople rather than anywhere else in the empire or in the eastern Mediterranean as a whole.

Byzantine religious ivories are icons, to be understood in the wider context of panel-painting, fresco and mosaic. Just as a famous icon would be often reproduced,[4] so ivories are made in multiple copies. The little triptych in Liverpool (No.17) is a modest version of the great triptychs in London, Paris and Berlin.[5] Scholars differ as to the extent of the classical repertoire used by Byzantine artists.[6] Some undoubtedly classical motifs were widely known. They occur in what are apparently secular caskets, ranging from the great Veroli casket, made for some princely patron,[7] to more routine productions (No.21), some wholly or partly in bone. The influence of the Byzantine tradition may be seen in the Magdeburg panels (Nos 11–13) and in the Anglo-Saxon Nativity (No.15). In two respects it differs from Ottonian and Romanesque work. Elephant ivory being more plentiful, there is no need to use the more limiting media of walrus ivory or whalebone. But the religious ivories, if not the secular, are far less inventive.

In 1261 the Palaeologan dynasty recovered Constantinople, restoring Byzantium to Greek control until the triumph of Islam in 1453. In these last centuries of the empire the artistic role of Constantinople within the eastern Mediterranean is not yet fully understood. Venice from the 11th century and Sicily in the 12th were indebted to the tradition of Byzantine art. Cyprus is still a treasury of Byzantine frescoes, some as old as the 12th century. But ivory-carving is another matter. From the late 13th century good-quality ivory was plentiful in Paris – but not, it would seem, in Constantinople. Our two 'Veneto-Byzantine' panels (No.22), with their uncertain credentials, highlight the unanswered questions. Was ivory available in the Byzantine empire, c.1250–1450? Was it used? If so, where were the centres of production?

1   In Rome the Byzantine artistic tradition persisted: see e.g. P. Romanelli and P.J. Nordhagen, *S. Maria Antiqua* (Rome, 1964).

2   Goldschmidt-Weitzmann II. See also Weitzmann's overview in his 'Ivory sculpture of the Macedonian Renaissance', in *Kolloquium über spätantike und frühmittelalterliche Skulptur: Heidelberg II, Vortragstexte 1970*, ed. V. Milojčić (Mainz, 1971), pp.1–12, reprinted in K. Weitzmann, *Classical Heritage in Byzantine and Near Eastern Art* (London, 1981).

3   I. Kalavrezou-Maxeiner, 'Dating the Romanos ivory', *Dumbarton Oaks Papers* 31 (1977), pp.307–25. She identifies the emperor as Romanos IV (1068–71). See now the judicious *mise-au-point* by D. Gaborit-Chopin in *Byzance* 148.

4   See No.20, note 1.

5   Goldschmidt-Weitzmann II.38, 39 and 72.

6   Contrast Weitzmann's assumption that the treasure-house of antique literature and art was still accessible with the cautious words of I. Kalavrezou-Maxeiner: 'Classical or antique subject-matter, in summary, survives in only a few formulas rather than as a subject-matter that is being revivified': 'The cup of San Marco and the "Classical" in Byzantium', in *Studien zur mittelalterlichen Kunst 800–1250: Festschrift für Florentine Mütherich zum 70. Geburtstag* (Munich, 1985), ed. K. Bierbrauer, P.K. Klein and W. Sauerländer, pp.167–74, at p.172.

7   J. Beckwith, *The Veroli Casket* (London, 1962).

16

Nativity and Crucifixion

10th–11th century   Byzantine

M 8019

Pls XVIa–b

Ivory. 126 × 113 × 9 mm.

Recto. Now lacks the frieze along the lower edge (see *Verso*). Two part-holes on the R edge; two holes to L and R of the angels in the *Nativity*, the R hole still plugged with ivory, the L hole empty and enlarged. Four later holes in top margin and above the *Crucifixion*, which is damaged at Christ's arms, Longinus' spear, Stephaton's L arm, reed and sponge, and the L of the lower edge, below the feet of the Maries. *Verso.* Lower frieze now cut to half its width, with the loss of 8 mm. along the lower edge. Traces of gilding in the Virgin's halo and at the top of the Cross.

Nativity. Swaddled Child with cruciform halo in crib centre, raised on stone pediment. Ox and ass above, and star in top centre with ray pointing to Child's head. To L the Virgin shows the Child to the Magi approaching from R. Joseph is seated far L. Above L an angel kneels behind the fold dividing heaven from earth. To R three crowded Magi present gifts. Above, a second angel addresses a shepherd (far R), two of whose sheep are below the crib. *Crucifixion.* Christ with Longinus (L) and Stephaton (R). To L the Virgin with two women, the first gesturing, the second weeping. To R John, with book in veiled hand; behind him Peter speaking with a servant, and for the third time denying Christ (Mark 14:70). *Verso.* (Pl.XVIb) Rectangle with narrow plain borders top and bottom; indistinct incised drawings in main space. Outer border a broad leaf-pattern frieze above and below; a further plain border all round.

One of a group of panels characterised by their foliate borders – Goldschmidt and Weitzmann's 'Rahmengruppe'. Two features of the *Nativity* recur in this group: the formalised star, and the two angels.[1] The intrusion of the Magi into the announcement to the shepherds is an infelicity not found elsewhere in the group. In the *Crucifixion* the Virgin leads the same group of women as subsequently visit the Sepulchre. To R, Peter's denial supplies two male figures behind St John. The panel has Byzantine elements (e.g. the angels) rather than being self-evidently Constantinopolitan. Arguably this is Venetian work, which could draw on both Western and Byzantine tradition. In the view of Goldschmidt and Weitzmann however 'the Byzantines have it'.[2]

Provenance. Acquired by Pulszky, apparently not from the Fejérváry collection.

Pulszky 39; Maskell, p.170 (erroneously described); Gatty 35; Graeven i.7; Nelson I, no.VII; BFAC 66; Longhurst, *Catalogue* I, p.45; Goldschmidt-Weitzmann II.215; *LI* 26; *MRT* 107.

---

1   Goldschmidt-Weitzmann II.197 (private collection in Paris) and 203 (Ravenna, Museo Bizantino).

2   Goldschmidt-Weitzmann II, pp.20–1.

Plate XVIa
Nativity and Crucifixion. (Reduced)

Plate XVIb
Leaf decoration on reverse. (Reduced)

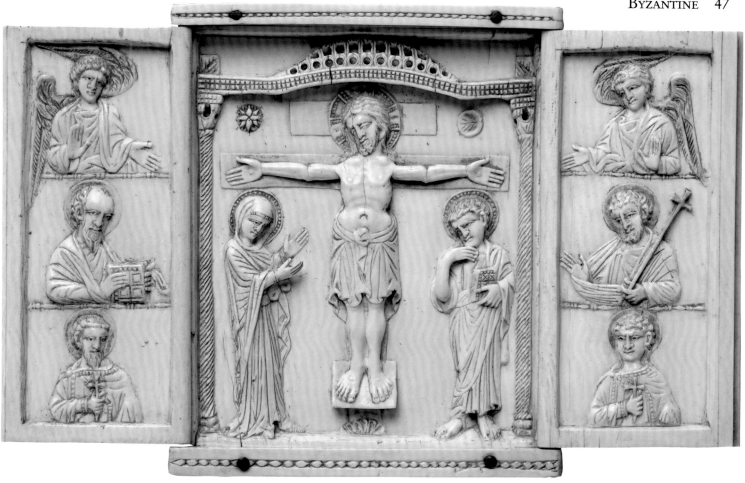

Plate XVIIa
Triptych of Crucifixion (open). (Reduced)

Plate XVIIb
Triptych of Crucifixion (closed). (Reduced)

17
Triptych of Crucifixion

10th–11th century   Constantinople

M 8063

Pls XVIIa–d (colour plates on previous page)

Ivory. 162 × 245 (129 closed) × 7 mm.
Each wing 142 × 64 mm.

Plate XVIIc
Central panel of Crucifixion triptych.
Kestner Museum, Hanover

Five pieces of ivory: central panel, upper and lower frame bars, wings. Repairs (19th-century) on the outer vertical edges of the wings. The central panel is attached to the upper and lower frame bars by metal nails. The wings are attached to the frame bars at their inner edge top and bottom, presumably by the original ivory pins. Extensive gilding on the central panel; gilding and blue in eyes of figures on R wing; gilding and blue pigment on verso.

Centre. Crucifixion with the Virgin (L) and St John (R). Sun (L) and moon (R) above; *tabula ansata* blank; below the *suppedaneum* a conche shell. The figures are framed by a baldachino supported by two spiral columns with acanthus capitals; there are vestigial palm-leaves above. *Left wing.* The archangel Michael (above), St Paul (centre) and St Theodore (below). *Right wing.* The archangel Gabriel above, St Peter (centre) and St George (below). This ivory lacks inscriptions, but the figures can be identified in that they conform to a standard series.[1] On the back of each wing a cross (Pl.XVIIb). The vertical diamond pattern at the edge of each wing is a 19th-century repair.

This is one of the few Byzantine triptychs to survive in its complete and original state, but for the replacement ivory on the wings. The other complete triptychs (Goldschmidt-Weitzmann II.38–9, 72) are bigger, iconographically more elaborate and of exceptionally high quality in their carving; they are display pieces, perhaps for a family chapel. The Liverpool triptych is much less ambitious: the carving is of only moderate quality, and elements of the design recur in some two dozen other scattered panels, each a

witness to a lost triptych. There is a striking parallel to the central panel in the Kestner Museum in Hanover (Pl.XVIIc) and again in Baltimore.[2] Two detached wings in the British Museum are iconographically almost identical (Pl.XVIId).[3] These triptychs were 'commercial'[4] productions such as were unknown in Western Europe before c.1300.

Provenance. Mayer collection by 1855.

Guardbook 35a; Waring, p.10; Gatty 31; Maskell, p.170; Graeven i.11–12; Nelson I, no.V; BFAC 58; Goldschmidt-Weitzmann II.155; *LI* 23; *MRT* 106.

---

1 Some examples have identifying inscriptions: see Goldschmidt-Weitzmann I, p.67.

2 Hanover, Kestner Museum 1893.2 and Baltimore, Walters Art Gallery 71.65 (=Randall 194): Goldschmidt-Weitzmann II.156 and 168 respectively. See also Kofler-Truniger S9: H. Schnitzler et al., *Mittelalterliche Elfenbein- und Emailkunst aus der Sammlung E. und M. Kofler-Truniger, Luzern* (Düsseldorf, 1965).

3 London, British Museum, MLA 1902.11–19.3: Goldschmidt-Weitzmann II.183.

4 Goldschmidt and Weitzmann speak of 'd(ie) gross(e) Gruppe der *Handelsware* des hieratischen Typus' (II, p.67, italics mine).

Plate XVIId
Wings of triptych. Trustees of the British Museum, London

Plate XVIII
Central panel of Crucifixion triptych

18

Central panel of a Crucifixion triptych

10th–11th centuries   Provincial Byzantine

M 8013

Pl.XVIII

Ivory. 151 × 97 × 5–6 mm.

Two original holes in the upper and lower margins to hold frame bars: see No.17. Another hole at the centre of the upper and lower margins. Wax repair to the centre of the upper margin and the baldachino below. The baldachino is damaged at its lower edge. Cracks throughout. Traces of gilding and blue pigment on St John's robe and Christ's halo.

Crucifixion with the Virgin (L) and St John (R). *Tabula ansata* lacking; below the *suppedaneum* a rock or an inverted conche shell. Angels to L and R of Christ's head; moon (L) and sun (R) above the baldachino. Plain columns with capitals and palm leaves support the baldachino; their bases are inverted capitals. A panel of poorer quality than No.17, but clearly in the same tradition. The column-bases, the rock / conche shell below the Cross, and the uncertain termination of the Cross behind Christ's halo indicate that the carver was out of touch with the best metropolitan work.[1]

Provenance. Fejérváry collection by 1855.

Henszlmann 672; Pulszky 45; Westwood 385 ('73.133); Gatty 32; Graeven i.9; Nelson I, no.VI; Goldschmidt-Weitzmann II.172; BFAC 59; *LI* 24; K. Weitzmann, 'Various aspects of Byzantine influence on the Latin countries from the sixth to the twelfth century', *Dumbarton Oaks Papers* 20 (1966), pp.3–24, at p.17, and fig.32, reprinted in *idem, Art in the Medieval West and its contacts with Byzantium* (London, 1982).

---

1   In the view of Goldschmidt and Weitzmann the panel could be 'western' (being of such poor quality). If so, the reversed position of sun and moon, which is occasionally found in Carolingian ivories and manuscript illumination, may be a further indicator.

Plate XIX
Central panel of Deesis triptych

19

Central panel of a Deesis triptych

10th–11th century   Byzantine

M 8020

Pl.XIX

Ivory. 146 × 108 × 6 mm.

Two original holes in the upper and lower margins to hold the frame bars: see No.17. A later hole just below the upper margin at centre. A severe crack on the R down the whole panel, and other minor cracks in the margin. Back: E.? L incised. RC 2 in silver, or oxidised red, paint (=Pulszky 1844).

Deesis. The Virgin and St John the Baptist intercede with Christ the Judge. Christ, barefoot (the Virgin and St John are shod), stands on a footstool; his R hand is raised in blessing, and he holds a book in his left. Above, St Peter (L), two angels with veiled hands (centre) touching Christ's halo, and St Paul (R). The intercession of the Virgin and St John the Baptist is an established image by the 6th century,[1] although the verbal term 'deesis' is not current before the mid-11th. Like Nos 17–18, the triptych to which this panel belonged served as a portable icon, a reminder of the larger painted panels: whether mounted on the dividing screen (iconostasis) in a church, or elsewhere in public buildings and in the home.

Provenance. Fejérváry collection by 1844, from Böhm in Vienna.

Pulszky 1844, Byz.3; Henszlmann 671; Pulszky 38; Gatty 33; Graeven i.6; BFAC 62; Goldschmidt-Weitzmann II.173; *LI* 25.

---

1 Th.von Bogyay, 'Deesis', in *Reallexikon zur Byzantinischen Kunst* (Stuttgart, 1966), i.1178–86. See further P.J. Nordhagen, 'S. Maria Antiqua: the frescoes of the seventh century', *Acta ad Archaeologiam et Artium Historiam Pertinentia* 8 (1978), 89–142, at pp.109–11 and pls.xxx–xxxi.

Plate XX
St John the Baptist

20

St John the Baptist

10th–11th century   Constantinople

M 8014

Pl.XX

Ivory. Height of surviving original 218 mm.

The figure of St John the Baptist (including his footstool and a section of the lower frame) has been skilfully mounted on an ivory background and frame, presumably in the 18th or 19th century, certainly by 1858 (Waring). The L side of the saint's face is badly damaged, and there are cracks at his L foot and the footstool below. The inscription on the scroll has traces of red.

John the Baptist, in a long tunic with decorated belt, a cloak of skins and sandals, gestures with his R hand, holding in his left a scroll: ΙΔΕ Ο ΑΜΝΟΣ ΤΟΥ ΘΕΟΥ Ο ΑΙΡΟΝ ΤΗΝ ΑΜΑΡΤΙΑΝ ΤΟΥ ΚΟΣΜΟΥ. ('Behold the Lamb of God, which taketh away the sin of the world': John 2:29.) The ivy-leaf at the end is a Late Antique formula that persists into Carolingian manuscripts: see for example London, BL, MS Add.24142, fol.70v (a Theodulf Bible). The figure has been cut from its original background (we do not know when) to be seen free-standing or, in candle-light, as a silhouette. Other examples of this treatment are three Virgins Hodegetria,[1] and the group now in Dumbarton Oaks: St John the Baptist, the Virgin and St Basil.[2] The Baptist was probably pointing to Christ. If so, the Liverpool figure belongs either to a Deesis, with the Baptist on the L,[3] or to a Hodegetria group as at Dumbarton Oaks. Given the surviving analogies, the Baptist is more likely to be pointing to the infant Christ in the arms of the Virgin Hodegetria than to Christ as Judge (cf.No.19). Stylistically the figure belongs to the 'Romanos' group: see chapter introduction above. The elegantly-inscribed scroll is unique in the corpus of Byzantine ivories.[4] Text-scrolls of this kind are increasingly common in German manuscript illumination of the later 11th and 12th centuries, illumination which may in turn reflect lost Byzantine models.

Provenance. Fejérváry collection by 1844, acquired from Böhm in Vienna.

Pulszky 1844, Byz.1; Henszlmann 670; Pulszky 44; Waring, p.11 (drawing); Maskell, pp.171–2; Westwood 175 ('58.27); J. Ruskin, 'The three colours of Pre-Raphaelitism', *The Nineteenth Century* 4 (1878), pp.1073–4; Gatty 28; Graeven i.10; Nelson I, no.VIII; BFAC 57; Goldschmidt-Weitzmann II.52; *LI* 21; *MRT* 104.

1   Goldschmidt-Weitzmann II.46, 48–9. The term 'Hodegetria' derives from the monastery τῶν ὁδηγῶν (lit. 'of the guides') in Constantinople, founded by the imperial family c.430 in the east of the city, looking towards the Bosporus. An icon in this monastery, showing the Virgin standing with the Child in her arms, was carried round the city walls during the Arab siege of 717. It was still the 'Victory' of Constantinople when Michael VIII reestablished Byzantine rule in 1261.

2   Weitzmann 26: pls xxxvii, xxxix and xl, color plate 6.

3   The Deesis with the Baptist on the R (as No.19) may be the earlier form, but there is also good 11th-century evidence for the Baptist on the L: Goldschmidt-Weitzmann II.69 (Paris: private collection) and 70 (Munich: Nationalmuseum).

See now Lons-le-Saunier, Musée des Beaux-Arts, C13, another 'silhouette' figure of the Baptist, also on the L, possibly the wing of a triptych: *Byzance* 152.

4   The script is mid-11th century at the latest, the accents and breathings being much later additions. I am indebted here to Professor Cyril Mango. The other ivory of St John the Baptist with the scriptural verse (but no scroll) is in St Petersburg: Goldschmidt-Weitzmann II.225. The Baptist with an inscribed scroll does occur in 12th-century mosaics: see two figures (both restored) in the north transept of the Cappella Palatina in Palermo: O. Demus, *The Mosaics of Norman Sicily* (London, 1950), pp.63 and 65 (notes 92 and 135), pls 12 and 21 and now E. Kitzinger, *La Cappella Palatina di Palermo: i mosaici del presbiterio*, I Mosaici del Periodo Normanno in Sicilia I, Accademia Nazionale di scienze lettere e arti di Palermo (Palermo, 1992), figs 22–4 and 93, 99–100.

Plate XXIa
Naked woman and warrior

Plate XXIb
Apollo and Hippolytus

Plate XXIc
Centaur

Plate XXId
Putto

Plate XXIe
Soldier with shield

Plate XXIf
Soldier with raised sword

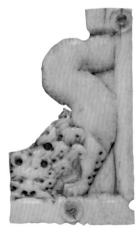

Plate XXIg
Man with serpent's tail

Plate XXIh
Lion

21

Eight casket panels

10th–11th century   Constantinople

M 8032–39

Pls XXIa–i

Bone.

1. M 8038: 62 × 58 × 3 mm.	5. M 8035: 51 × 44 × 1 mm.
2. M 8039: 62 × 55 × 2 mm.	6. M 8036: 62 × 48 × 2 mm.
3. M 8037: 59 × 46 × 2 mm.	7. M 8032: 60 × 34 × 2 mm.
4. M 8034: 60 × 49 × 3 mm.	8. M 8033: 60 × 34 × 2 mm.

All the panels have (or had) four holes in the upper and lower borders to attach them to the wooden framework of a casket. Following the Goldschmidt-Weitzmann reconstruction, the square panels (1–2) are from the lid, the vertical rectangles (3–6) from the sides and ends, while the last two (7–8) flanked the keyhole on the front. All are in varying degrees damaged.

1 (Pl.XXIa) *naked woman* (L), with torch in her R hand and cloak in her L, is greeted by *warrior* with spear in his L hand, making chin-chucking gesture with his R.[1] (M 8038)

2 (Pl.XXIb) *Apollo* (L), seated and naked to the waist, strums his lyre. To R, *Hippolytus*, naked, carrying a spear in his L hand, raises his R hand to address Phaedra (not shown).[2] (M 8039)

3 (Pl.XXIc) *centaur*, with raised sword in R hand and shield in L, cloak flying behind.[3] (M 8037)

4 (Pl.XXId) *putto*, bearded, blowing horn; his cloak flies behind. (M 8034)

5 (Pl.XXIe) *soldier* with *shield* in L hand and scabbard at his back. (M 8035)

6 (Pl.XXIf) *soldier* with *raised sword* in R hand and shield (with strap dangling) in his L.[4] (M 8036)

7 (Pl.XXIg) *man* looking R, with *serpent's tail*, ending in a beast's head. (M 8032)

8 (Pl.XXIh) *lion* looking directly forward, with *serpent's tail*. (M 8033)

These panels reflect the fashion for Greek mythology and 'classical' style in the Byzantine court from the mid-10th century to the later 11th. This aristocratic art may be seen at its best in the Veroli casket in the Victoria & Albert Museum (Pl.XXIi).[5] At the lower and more routine level of bone carving, the Liverpool panels follow the Veroli casket in style and iconography (cf. Pl.XXIa). A casket in Bologna is a complete example from the same workshop, indicating that affordable duplicates – or even multiple copies – might be made of a *tour de force* in ivory.[6] What remains to be clarified is the degree to which ivory and bone were combined, and how far the original design included colour and / or gilding.[7]

Provenance. Fejérváry collection by 1855.

Henszlmann 682; Pulszky 58–65; Maskell, p.172; Gatty 38; Graeven i.13; BFAC 52; Goldschmidt-Weitzmann I.30; *LI* 22; J. Beckwith, *The Veroli Casket* (London, 1962); *MRT* 105.

Plate XXIi

Veroli casket, detail. Courtesy of the Board of Trustees of the Victoria & Albert Museum, London

---

1 Cf. the Veroli casket, R of panel (Pl.XXIi); also No.42, the same gesture in a completely different milieu.

2 See K. Weitzmann, 'Euripides scenes in Byzantine art', *Hesperia* 18 (1949), 159–210, at 192; *idem*, 'Probleme der mittelbyzantinischen Renaissance', *Jahrbuch des deutschen archäologischen Instituts* 48, Archäologischer Anzeiger 1933, pp.338–60, at 344: both reprinted in *idem*, *Classical Heritage in Byzantine and Near Eastern Art* (London, 1981). For Apollo, see *idem*, *Greek Mythology in Byzantine Art*, *Studies in Manuscript Illumination* 4 (Princeton, 1951), pp.174–7 and fig.219. See also the parallel in a casket in the Museo Nazionale in Florence: I. Kalavrezou-Maxeiner, 'The cup of San Marco and the 'Classical' in Byzantium', in *Studien zur mittelalterlichen Kunst 800–1250: Festschrift für Florentine Mütherich zum 70. Geburtstag* (Munich, 1985), ed. K. Bierbrauer, P.K. Klein and W. Sauerländer, pp.167–74, at p.172 and fig.7, citing Goldschmidt-Weitzmann I.24.

3 Weitzmann, 1951 (note 2 above), p.182 and fig.241.

4 For 5 and 6 cf. a casket in the Metropolitan Museum of Art, New York: Kalavrezou-Maxeiner, *op.cit.* pp.171–2 and fig.5, citing Goldschmidt-Weitzmann I.12.

5 London, Victoria & Albert Museum, 216–1865: Goldschmidt-Weitzmann I.21.

6 The case for multiple copies in bone is cogently argued by A. Cutler, 'On Byzantine boxes', *Journal of the Walters Art Gallery* 42–3 (1984–85), 32–47.

7 See the pioneering study by Carolyn L. Connor, 'New perspectives on Byzantine ivories', *Gesta* 30 (1991), 100–11. Dr Connor points out that in a mixed object of ivory and bone colour would mask the joins in the bone, and even distract attention from the use of bone altogether.

Plates XXIIa–b
Veneto–Byzantine panels, showing two angels

Plates XXIIc–d
Crosses on the reverse

22

Two angels on panels

Purportedly 14th century, but perhaps 19th century   Veneto–Byzantine

1986.227.1

Pls XXIIa–d

Ivory. L wing 80 × 39 × 5 mm.;
R wing 80 × 42 × 5 mm.

Each panel has a hole top centre and is damaged at or near the lower edge. Though united now as a diptych, the panels do not match. They are considered too fragile to permit radio-carbon dating.

L panel, recto. Angel with veiled hands in plain frame. The upper border is divided by a horizontal line; in the lower border a similar line does duty as the ground on which the angel stands. *Verso.* Cross, with circle above and below main vertical. *R panel, recto.* Angel as L panel, differing slightly in stance and expression. The R edge of the border canted outwards. *Verso.* as L panel.

It would be easy, and perhaps prudent, to dismiss these panels as 19th-century copies of a half-understood Byzantine original. The angels' headgear, their expressions, the fact that (as angels) they stand on the ground at all, the circles above the crosses on the verso: all these features are disquieting. On the other hand, the history of Byzantine ivory-carving after the Palaeologan return (1261), and in provincial workshops has yet to be written. If these angels are genuinely 14th-century, that is where they belong.

Provenance. Up Holland College, Lancashire; sold Christie's 15 July 1986.

4

Romanesque

Romanesque Europe had no secure supply of ivory, and thus no established workshop practice. In southern Italy and Sicily, and to some extent in Spain, the situation was better: witness the S. Denis chessmen and the great antependium now in Salerno.[1] But this Mediterranean tradition seems to have had no direct effect on either the technique or the imagery of northern carving in ivory and bone. In the North, the most striking achievement is in walrus ivory: Mosan portable altars, the Lewis chessmen and the Bury St Edmunds cross.[2] The last in particular is a *tour de force*.

By contrast the Liverpool pieces are modest solutions to routine problems of material and design: the best use of a fragment of ivory (No.23), the adaptation of the iconography of manuscript illumination to the medium of bone and whalebone (Nos 24–5) and the commercial provision of liturgical boxes and reliquaries (No.26).

---

1 Goldschmidt IV.161–74; IV.126.
2 Goldschmidt II.104–5; IV.182–239. For the Bury cross see Gaborit-Chopin 6–8.

23

Martyr

Second half of 11th century   Cologne

M 8232

Pl.XXIII

Ivory. 57 × 48 × 6–7 mm.

Plate XXIII
Martyr

A later hole top centre, otherwise in good condition.

A martyr, bearded, with a band round his hair, wearing a garment with beading round the sleeves, stands above the clouds of heaven. He carries a palm in his L hand and has his greatly-enlarged R hand raised in blessing. A frame of beading within acanthus. Perhaps from the R corner of a luxury binding.

Goldschmidt has set the Liverpool panel in the context of four other panels with similar borders, and a chess-piece.[1] Of these, the Berlin panel (now lost) patently reflects the coronation of St Gereon panel in Cologne, while the chess-piece was excavated in Cologne. The Maihingen-Wallerstein panel (now in Schloss Harburg) in the same group is cut on the verso of a Virgin *Hodegetria*. Thus the workshop which produced the group demonstrably had access to Byzantine models and – judging by 'the clouds of heaven' – Ottonian manuscript illumination.[2]

Provenance. Acquired by Joseph Mayer before 1855.[3]

Guardbook 35b; Gatty 37; Graeven i.7; Goldschmidt II.82; BFAC 45; *LI* 28; Beckwith 73 (proposing St Albans or Bury St Edmunds, second quarter of the 12th century).

---

1   Goldschmidt II.78–80; II, pp.8–9 and 35.

2   See for example the Hildesheim *Book of Collects* of *c.*1010–30: H. Mayr-Harting, *Ottonian Book Illumination*, 2 vols (London, 1991), i, plates XIV and XV.

3   For Mayer's continental visits see *Joseph Mayer*, p.4, with references.

24

Vintage scenes

*c.*1100   ?Northern French

M 8018

Pl.XXIV

Bone. 48 × 146 × 5 mm.

Plate XXIV
Vintage scenes

Later holes top L and bottom R; the border slightly chipped bottom L and L of top centre.

Two men with staves carry a basket of grapes from the vineyard, vines being shown far L and behind the basket. In a vaulted cellar, with a human mask as a roof-boss, a third man (R) rests two capacious wooden jugs on a barrel. A fourth man, seated far R, tastes the new wine. On the wall a basket of fruit and a shelf with two horn or leather bottles; on the floor a large pitcher with a handle.[1] An undecorated border.

A scene in the ancient calendrial tradition of the Labours of the Months, here September or October.[2] Although such secular scenes may well have been quite common in aristocratic household furniture, in the medium of ivory and bone the rate of survival is very low. Precedents may be sought in Middle Byzantine casket-panels and manuscript illumination.[3] Goldschmidt located the piece east of the Rhine, by analogy with a rather different casket, formerly in Berlin.[4] Lasko (*LI* 29) and Alexander (*MRT* 109) find a French provenance, again without a wholly convincing context.[5]

Provenance. Fejérváry collection by 1855.[6]

Henszlmann 668; Pulszky 40; Maskell, p.171; Westwood 345 ('73.108); Gatty 36; Graeven i.6; Goldschmidt II.174; BFAC 48; *LI* 29; *MRT* 109.

---

1   For such domestic receptacles in the 12th and 13th centuries see *English Romanesque Art 1066–1200*, Hayward Gallery, exhibition catalogue (London, 1984), pp.350–5, with references.

2   J.C. Webster, *The Labors of the Months in antique and medieval art* (Evanston / Chicago, 1938), pp.175–9.

3   Goldschmidt-Weitzmann I.67 (June: man mowing) and cf.I.27.

4   Goldschmidt II.173. This has quite elaborate borders, religious subject-matter, and stiffer and flatter figures and draperies.

5   The late 11th-century illuminated initial of 'the Vintage' (Rouen, Bibliothèque Municipale, MS 498, fol.60v, from Préaux) cited in *MRT* 109 is not a specific analogy. See *Trésors des Abbayes Normandes*, exhibition catalogue (Rouen / Caen, 1979), no.130.

6   Not in Pulszky 1844.

Plate XXVa
Presentation in the Temple (centre), *with four Old Testament scenes*

25

Presentation in the Temple

Mid-twelfth century   ?English

M 8016

Pls XXVa–e

Whalebone.[1] 204 × 98 × 9 mm.

Casket lid, with two hinge-slots R. The plain border is several mm. below the carved surface; presumably a strip of gilded metal was attached to it by the thirty or so nail-holes now visible, thus bringing it flush with the lid.

In the *central* scene (Schorr, *passim*) the Virgin (L) presents the infant Christ to the aged Simeon, who receives him with veiled hands (R) and Anna, identified 'ANa' on the skirt of her gown (far R) (Luke 2:22–39). Joseph follows (far L) with two doves, and anonymous members of the crowd are in shallow relief (L and R). The Temple architecture, supported by four spiral columns, is a triple baldachino in the Byzantine manner. The four smaller scenes top and bottom are: *top L*, Moses receiving the tablets of the Law on Mount Sinai (Exod.31:18) – note unexplained star and witnesses; *top R*, Abraham about to sacrifice Isaac, prevented by the Hand of God (R), with angel providing ram (L) (Gen.22:1–14); *bottom L*, Abel presents his offering of a lamb (Gen.4:2–5); *bottom R*, Melchizedek, king of Jerusalem, brings bread and wine to the conquering Abraham (Gen.14:18–20). Again anonymous bystanders in shallow relief bottom L and R. The

scenes have plain frames set within beading; an acanthus frame is round the whole panel.[2]

The four Old Testament scenes are antitypes of future Christian events: figures foreshadowing the reality to come. The Old Law of Moses prefigures the New Law which Christ will expound and fulfil. Abraham's readiness to sacrifice his only son prefigures the Crucifixion, the actual sacrifice of the son of God. The 'righteous' Abel (Heb.11:4), whose offering was accepted by God, balances Melchizedek, whose bread and wine prefigures the Eucharist. Only two of the four Old Testament protagonists have haloes. It is characteristic of the mid-12th century that the schematic relation of these scenes is slightly unsteady. Although all are broadly appropriate, none is 'necessary', in the organised, rigorous manner of the next generation. Then the sacrifice of Abraham would be directly, plainly juxtaposed to the Crucifixion.[3]

Beckwith has attributed the panel to 'the school of Canterbury'. Although too little ivory and bone carving survives to

Plate XXVb
Abel and Melchizedek mosaic in San Vitale, Ravenna.
Photograph courtesy of the estate of E.A. Remnant, London

Plate XXVc
Abraham and Melchizedek illumination in a manuscript of the Psychomachia. By permission of the British Library, London

Plate XXVd
Abraham scenes in the Fulda Sacramentary.
Staatsbibliothek, Bamberg

reconstruct a workshop, some details of the iconography do derive from the kind of antique models which could have been known at Canterbury.[4] These are most notably the rendering of Abel, which is closely matched in a 6th-century mosaic in San Vitale, Ravenna (Pl.XXVb);[5] and the triangular stamp on Melchizedek's loaf of bread.[6] How these formulae were transmitted – whether by sculpture or manuscript illumination – we do not fully understand. One route may well be the antique cycle of illustrations to the *Psychomachia* of Prudentius, Carolingian versions of which show Abraham presenting a lamb to Melchizedek (Pl.XXVc).[7] This is the tithe due from the secular warrior, Abraham, to the priestly figure of Melchizedek.[8] There is precedent too for both Abraham scenes in the Fulda Sacramentary (Pl.XXVd),[9] and rather strikingly for the central Presentation scene in the *Codex Egberti* (Pl.XXVe).[10]

Provenance. Acquired by Fejérváry in Ghent pre-1844.

Pulszky 1844, Medieval 1; Henszlmann 667; Pulszky 42; Maskell, App.p.170; Westwood 266 ('73.73); Gatty 34; Graeven i.8; R. Stettiner, *Die illustrierten Prudentiushandschriften* (Berlin, 1905), pl.38; Goldschmidt IV.70; BFAC 77; D.C. Schorr, 'The iconographic development of the Presenta-

Plate XXVe
Presentation scene in the Codex Egberti. Stadtbibliothek, Trier

tion in the Temple', *Art Bulletin* 28 (1946), 17–32, at pp.17–25 and figs 1–15; *LI* 30; Beckwith 102, ill.204, pp.140–1; *MRT* 110; *English Romanesque Art 1066–1200* (London, Hayward Gallery, exhibition catalogue 1984) 219.

---

1   *Pace* Beckwith 102, not walrus ivory.

2   The panel is a single piece of whalebone, cut to give the effect of five panels slotted into a frame.

3   See for example H. Buschhausen, *Der Verduner Altar: das Emailwerk des Nikolaus von Verdun im Stift Klosterneuburg* (Vienna, 1980), pp.52–6.

4   Nor need the provenance be restricted to Canterbury on the ground of antique models; Winchester is at least as likely a source of similar material.

5   F.W. Deichmann, *Ravenna: Hauptstadt des spätantiken Abendlandes*, 6 vols (Stuttgart, 1958–89), i, pl.314.

6   See G. Galavaris, *Bread and the Liturgy: the symbolism of early Christian and Byzantine bread stamps* (Madison / Milwaukee / London, 1970), caps 2–3, at pp.32–3 (signifying the Trinity) *et passim*.

7   See for example London, BL, MS Add.24199, from Bury St Edmunds (first half of the 11th century). The classic discussion of the pictures is R. Stettiner, *Die illustrierten Prudentiushandschriften*, dissertation volume and plates volume (Berlin, 1895 and 1905); see further H. Woodruff, *The Illustrated Manuscripts of Prudentius* (Cambridge, 1930). The early and quite extensive gloss still awaits a modern editor. Melchizedek (it runs) 'sacerdos dictus est . . . quia ipse panem et uinum deo obtulit. non hostias de uictimis taurorum aut pecudum. Vnde iam

presignabat mutationem legalis sacerdotii. In nouo enim testamento sacrificium uictimarum translatum est in sacrificium corporis et sanguinis Christi': BL Add.24199, fol.3v.

8   In the juxtaposition of the two scenes the original identification of Abel is lost, perhaps by an early confusion of abbreviated names. Note also that Gen.14:20, 'And he gave him tithes of all', has reversed its meaning: now it is Abraham who pays Melchizedek.

9   Bamberg, Staatsbibliothek, MS lit.1 (A.II.52), fol.13 (997 / 1014): see H. Mayr-Harting, *Ottonian Book Illumination*, 2 vols (London, 1991), ii.144–5; H. Hoffmann, *Buchkunst und Königtum im ottonischen und frühsalischen Reich*, 2 vols (Stuttgart, 1986), i.139–40; E.H. Zimmermann, 'Fuldaer Buchmalerei', *Kunstgeschichtliches Jahrbuch der KK Zentral-Kommission für Kunst und historische Denkmale* (1910), 1–104. See notably too Göttingen, Universitätsbibliothek, MS theol.231, fol.1v (Mayr-Harting, ii, colour plate XII), from Fulda 970 / 75, which juxtaposes the two Abraham scenes horizontally.

10   Trier, Stadtbibliothek, MS 24, fol.18 (977 / 93): Mayr-Harting, *op.cit.*, ii.70–81; Hoffmann, *op.cit.*, i.488–9. See usefully E. Lucchesi Palli, 'Darbringung Jesu im Tempel', in Herder's *Lexikon des Christlichen Ikonographie*, 8 vols (1968–76), i.473–8. Note the common ground between the *Codex Egberti* and the Magdeburg ivories: Gibson, *op.cit.* (Nos 11–13 above).

Plate XXVIa
Evangelists box (Matthew and John)

Plate XXVIb
Evangelists box (Mark and Luke)

26
Evangelists box

First half of the 13th century   Cologne

M 8065

Pls XXVIa–f

Bone. 44 × 64 × 37 mm.

In three pieces: base, side showing the symbols of Matthew and John, and side showing the symbols of Mark and Luke.[1] Each holds his gospel in his hands, claws, paws or hooves. The four nails still in place on the exterior of the base secured nothing. The little box may once have been glued together; now the two sides are joined vertically at both edges with twisted wire. The ill-fitting lid may be modern, the finial certainly is. The inscriptions are filled with black mastic, the figures have traces of gilding and red paint.

The context of the evangelist symbols is the workshop(s) in Cologne in the early 13th century which produced circular or octagonal reliquary boxes with saints and apostles in the lower register, and cherubim and evangelist symbols above (Pl.XXVIc).[2] All this work was in bone, with the type of inscriptions and colouring described above. In one other instance the evangelist symbols are independent, constituting the box itself (Pl.XXVId);[3] but normally they are elements in a larger whole (Pl.XXVIe–f).[4] It is thus not impossible that M 8065 was originally two disparate sections, which at a later date were glued to a base, and finally (in the 19th century?) supplied with a lid.

Plate XXVIc
Octagonal reliquary made in Cologne.
Hessisches Landesmuseum, Darmstadt

Plate XXVId
Evangelists box made in Cologne.
Hessisches Landesmuseum, Darmstadt

Plates XXVIe–f
Evangelist panels. Hessisches Landesmuseum, Darmstadt

Provenance. Acquired by Joseph Mayer before 1855.

Guardbook 113; Maskell, p.172; Gatty 46; Graeven i.5; Goldschmidt III.79; BFAC 80 (doubting the authenticity); *LI* 31; *MRT* 113.

---

1 *Pace* Goldschmidt III.79, there is no wood in this box.

2 Darmstadt, Hessisches Landesmuseum, Kg 54: 228 (Goldschmidt III.70); well illustrated by A. von Euw, *Elfenbeinarbeiten von der Spätantike bis zum hohen Mittelalter* (Frankfurt-am-Main, 1976), no.25. See further *idem*, in *Rhein und Maas: Kunst und Kultur 800–1400*, 2 vols, Schnütgen-Museum (Cologne, 1973), ii.377–86, at pp.384 and 386.

3 Darmstadt, Hessisches Landesmuseum, Kg 54: 229 (Goldschmidt III.65); von Euw, no.29.

4 Darmstadt, Hessisches Landesmuseum, Kg 54: 224a–b; von Euw, no.28.

5
Gothic

Material. By the late 13th century good-quality elephant ivory was readily available in western Europe. Where it came from, and how and why it came when it did, is still uncertain in the details: but in principle the trade in ivory 'shadowed' the trade in gold. By 1250 gold coinage was returning to Europe after a lapse of half a millenium,[1] and ivory followed. The supply route ran up through Islamic Africa to Tunis, and thence into the established network of Mediterranean trade.[2] The principal workshops were in Paris itself.[3] In Paris the court of Philip the Fair (1285–1314) no doubt gave a lead to fashion; England followed, and to the north and east, in the lands of the Meuse and lower Rhine – perhaps notably Cologne,[4] cities and prince-bishoprics advertised their political independence by the luxury of their patronage. That said, it is still remarkable that Gothic ivory-carving – however flourishing – was restricted to so limited an area of northern Europe, bypassing Spain, Italy and southern France.

Religious ivories. The majority of Gothic ivories are diptych-panels or writing-tablets, normally within the measurements of *c.*200 × *c.*100 mm. Consisting of scenes from the New Testament, the life of the Virgin,[5] and representations of saints, they relate primarily to the Mass: Christ's nature, his Passion and resurrection, the interceding Virgin and saints. Iconographically it is a complete change from the complexities of Romanesque art: no Old Testament scenes, no scenes of Christ's ministry, no typology. This is a world of pattern-books and repetition of figures and familiar scenes (Nos 28, 30 and 32). But Crucifixion panels apart, no two surviving Gothic ivories are exact duplicates: at best, a six-scene diptych will be matched in another panel or diptych for three of its scenes and in yet a third panel for one or two more. However routine these Gothic panels may appear now, they are likely to have been specifically ordered by a patron (from a limited range of options) rather than speculatively produced for casual customers.

Secular ivories. Caskets (Nos 41–2), mirror cases (No.40) and combs (No.43) – essential items on a lady's dressing-table – are the first secular ivories to survive in any quantity since Late Antiquity.[6] Iconographically they are a very curious and enlightening mixture. A good number of scenes reflect the Arthurian cycle, the romance of Alexander and 'classical gossip' about Socrates and Aristotle.[7] The Castle of Love (No.40) is repeated from casket to casket to mirror case. A lady elopes with her knight from the castle, a little boat waiting in the moat below with an oarsman and a musician. Another day the same castle is assaulted by knights with ropes and ladders, and defended by ladies throwing roses from the battlements, while a tournament goes on in the yard.[8] These are the set-pieces of late medieval and Renaissance festivals, which 'leave not a wrack behind'.

1   Gold ceased to be minted in Gaul after the 670s. Frederick II's gold 'augustale' of 1231 was followed by St Louis' gold écu. See conveniently P. Grierson, *The Coins of Medieval Europe* (London, 1991), pp.25, 109–15.

2   For the gold trade see N. Levtzion, *Ancient Ghana and Mali* (London, 1973), cap.XII. I am much indebted here to Dr Murray Last, of University College, London.

3   The most specific guide is the *Livre des métiers*, a comprehensive list of the guilds that were permitted and active in mid-13th century Paris: R. de Lespinasse and F. Bonnardot, *Le livre des métiers d'Etienne Boileau*, Histoire Générale de Paris (Paris, 1879). Artisans were classified by their product, rather than by the material in which they worked. Five trades used ivory, none exclusively: cutlers (combs and knife-handles: cap.xvii), tailor's accessories (buttons, buckles: cap.xlii), image carvers (crucifixes and knife-handles: cap.lxi–lxii), makers of writing-tablets (cap.lxviii) and makers of chessmen and dice (cap.lxxi). We should not think in terms of one atelier working in ivory, another in wood and yet another in brass.

4   The tradition of ivory and bone carving had persisted there through the 12th century well into the 13th: see No.26 above and Goldschmidt III.61–81.

5   That is, the Infancy and Passion of Christ, plus the Dormition and Coronation of the Virgin herself.

6   The great exception is the *cathedra Petri* or throne of Charles the Bald: Gaborit-Chopin, 90–4.

7   D.J.A. Ross, 'Allegory and Romance on a mediaeval French marriage casket', *Journal of the Warburg and Courtauld Institutes* 11 (1948), pp.112–42.

8   For the casket-lids see W.D. Wixom, 'Eleven additions to the Medieval Collection', *Bulletin of the Cleveland Museum of Art* (1979), pp.86–151, at 110–26. Fine mirror-cases in the same tradition are Baltimore, Walters Art Gallery, 71.169 and 170 (Randall 322–3) and Seattle, Art Museum Fr.10.1 (Calkins 81).

27

Christ with Instruments of the Passion; Crucifixion; Virgin and Child: central panel of triptych

1280–1300   English

M 8011

Pls XXVIIa–b

Ivory. 121 × 62 × 8 mm.

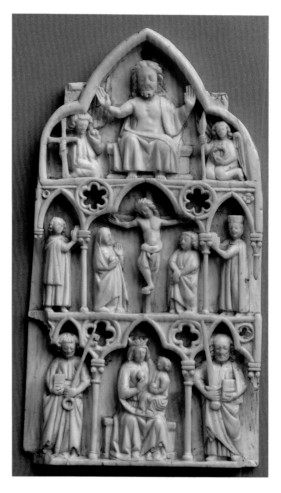

Plate XXVIIa
Central panel of triptych, showing Christ with Instruments of the Passion; Crucifixion; Virgin and Child

Presumably ring-hinges, now lost. The carving technique is somewhat crude and may indicate a provincial shop. Pinnacles may have been present on the shoulders of the piece: see the bases to L and R. The outer colonnettes (bottom) and tracery (L bottom) are damaged. A hole has been pierced at the top. Traces of red pigment on L edge; green staining in background areas between figures.

Three registers. Top. Christ displaying his wounds. On each side, an angel with Instruments of the Passion: L, holding cross and ?nails; R, holding spear and crown of thorns. *Middle.* Christ on the cross, with Mary and John; in side niches standing male (L) and female (R) donors in contemporary dress. *Bottom.* Virgin, with Child possibly crowning Virgin, each holding an orb (? fruit); in side niches, St Peter (L), with book and elongated key and St Paul (R), with book and upturned sword. At the top, a trefoil frame; middle and bottom registers in an architectural colonnade of three arches (middle arch trefoiled and wider); tracery sextfoil (middle) and quatrefoil (bottom) roundels in spandrels.

Christ as judge, seated, with body partly exposed, between angels with Instruments of the Passion is not uncommon in the second half of the 13th century (cf. Koechlin 43; Gaborit-Chopin, figs 214, 216). The figure is unusual at this period in having *both* hands raised, as in some book illustration (Morgan II.166, 167); by the first quarter of the 14th century this iconography was more generally adopted in ivory work (see e.g. Koechlin 234, 265, 348bis). A seated or standing Virgin may often be placed below the Crucifixion; the image is more conventionally shown with angel figures at the side, but a later 14th-century triptych in the Metropolitan Museum of Art, New York also shows Peter and Paul on side leaves beside a central crowned Virgin (Koechlin 52).[1]

The Child's anticipatory gesture towards the Virgin's crown is rare, as are figures of donors, especially in a standing posture. The male donor appears to wear a surcote of the garde-corps type of the mid-13th century; the female's headdress consists of a barbette and filet, worn in the 13th and early 14th centuries.[2] A comparable panel, of good English provenance, is London, Victoria & Albert Museum, 747–1877 (Pl.XXVIIb).

Provenance. Fejérváry collection by 1855.

Henszlmann 675; Pulszky 47; Westwood 393 ('73.139); Maskell, p.172; Gatty 45; BFAC 102; Koechlin 60 and I, p.90, note 3 (not English); Longhurst, no.LIV; Longhurst, *Catalogue*, pl.II; Natanson, *Gothic* 22; *LI* 32; *MRT* 114; Porter 29 and pp.90–3; *Age of Chivalry: art in Plantagenet England 1200–1400*, 6 November 1987 – 6 March 1988, exhibition catalogue ed. J. Alexander and P. Binski (London, 1987).

Plate XXVIIb
Crucifixion; Virgin and Child. Courtesy of the Board of Trustees of the Victoria & Albert Museum, London

---

1   See also the triptych (now London, British Museum, *MLA* 61.4–4.16, *Age of Chivalry* 593) made for John de Grandisson, bishop of Exeter, in which SS Peter and Paul flank a Coronation of the Virgin.

2   C. Willett and P. Cunningham, *Handbook of English Mediaeval Costume* (London, 1952), pp.42–3, 50, 52, 54.

28

Diptych of the Life and Passion of Christ

1350–70   Paris

M 8006

Pls XXVIIIa–c

Ivory. 189 × 242 (including hinges) × 9 mm.; width of each leaf 119 mm.

Plate XXVIIIa
Diptych of the Life and Passion of Christ. (Reduced)

Two hinges.

Two registers. Scenes from the Infancy and Passion cycles: *below L*, 1. Annunciation, with standing figures, lily pot, and dove descending; 2. Nativity and Announcement to Shepherds, with Child in manger beside bed; Joseph, seated, gesturing, with cane; *below R*, 3. Adoration of the Magi, one King pointing to Star. The Christ Child is standing, blessing, and reaching in goblet; the Virgin holds his trailing gown; 4. Entry into Jerusalem, with Zacchaeus in tree, man putting down his cloak, figure with drapery raised above his head,

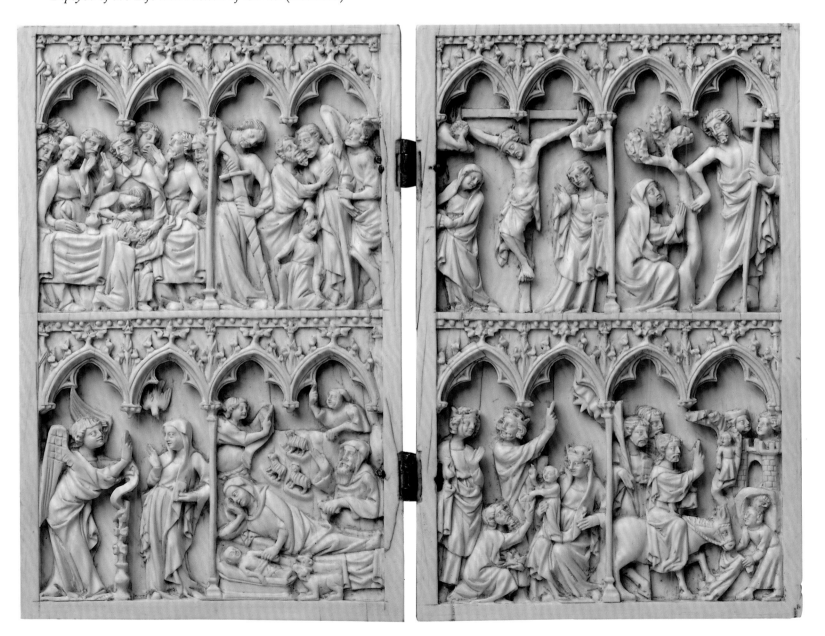

and Apostle behind Christ holding book and palm; *above L*, 5. Last Supper, with the Apostles taking bread, and, kneeling apart, Judas receiving sop from Christ; 6. Betrayal; *above R*, 7. Christ on the Cross, with Mary, John, and angels above mourning; 8. *Noli me tangere*: Mary Magdalen kneeling by Christ, who holds a crossed staff; tree between figures. Architectural setting for each scene an arcade of four trefoiled arches decorated with leafy crockets and finials and sup-

ported by a single colonnette at the centre. Above, a moulding with a row of beading.

This disposition of eight scenes may represent a revision of an arrangement of four registers on each leaf (Koechlin 34–7). The composition and iconography, including the conflation of the Nativity and Announcement, are typical of this period; even the charming detail of the Virgin reaching out to touch the Child is conventional. The Virgin's head-in-hand posture

Plates XXVIIIb and c (opposite)
Two panels set in the St Denis binding. Musée du Louvre, Paris

was a common sign to indicate sloth, grief, sleep or contemplation (here the last).[1] Several scenes can be closely matched elsewhere. The Annunciation, Adoration of the Magi and the Entry into Jerusalem may be compared with a diptych now in Brussels (Koechlin 370); and the selection and positioning of six scenes, the arcade supported by a single colonnette, and some aspects of the iconography are similar to a diptych of the later 14th century in the Walters Art Gallery (71.273:

Randall 304).[2] The Entry, the Betrayal and the *Noli me tangere* appear in the two panels set in the binding of a treasure of St. Denis, the Greek text of Denis the Areopagite (Pls XXVIIIb–c).[3]

Provenance. Fejérváry collection by 1855.

Henszlmann 678; Pulszky 53–4; Westwood 412–13 ('73.147–50); Maskell, pp.172–3; Gatty 49; Cust, p.145, fig.32 (L panel); Nelson II, no.XVII; BFAC 114; Koechlin 369; *LI* 38.

Plate XXVIIIc

---

1   It is found in many Adoration and other scenes: e.g. Nos 29, 30, 32. See further F.P. Pickering, *Literature and Art in the Middle Ages* (Coral Gables, Florida, 1970), pp.93–7; K.L. Scott, 'The Illustrations of *Piers Plowman* in Bodleian Library MS Douce 104', *The Yearbook of Langland Studies* 4 (1990), pp.1–86, at pp.17–19, 47–9, 59.

2   Randall notes that the Walters piece is one of a group of 'diptychs with colonnettes' that are 'consistent in style . . . conventional in repertoire' and often 'rough in workmanship'. No.28 is in some respects similar, but the drapery and two pictorial subjects differ, and there is no beading on the Walters frame.

3   Paris, Louvre, Objets d'Art MS MR 416 (1403–5 AD: sc. date of the binding, not date of the ivories); Koechlin 823. See *Le Trésor de Saint-Denis*, Musée du Louvre 12 Mars – 17 Juin 1991 (Paris, 1991), pp.278–81, with references.

Plate XXIX
Diptych of the Life and Passion of Christ; Coronation of the Virgin

29

Diptych of the Life and Passion of Christ; Coronation of the Virgin

Mid-14th century   ?Rhine – Meuse

M 8049

Pl.XXIX

Ivory. 178 × 196 (two panels) × 9 mm.

Three hinges intact. The diptych, which is in good repair, has never been painted.

Two registers. Infancy and Passion scenes: *below L*, 1. Annunciation, with lily pot, conflated with 2. Nativity, with Joseph seated beside, gesturing, with cane; *below R*, 3. Adoration of the Magi; *above L*, 4. Crucifixion, with (L) swooning Virgin supported by two Maries, at R, two men in Jews' hats and a mourner; *above R*, 5. Coronation of the Virgin, with angels censing, holding Cloth of Honour behind, and crowning. Triple arcading above and below.

This diptych is stylistically and iconographically unusual. The style is characterised by sinuous, flowing lines, with broader open folds of drapery or other open space. Koechlin and Lasko both noted the iconographic detail of the Virgin reclining on a bed in the Adoration scene as a theme rare before the 15th century. In the same scene the Child is standing and twisting back in a *contraposto* attitude. The gift presented in a goblet with a lid held open by the king is also an unusual feature, as is the crown slipped over the arm of the leading king. The Virgin supports the Christ Child in a playful manner, by a girdle round his waist, as he leans towards the gift. The 'half' Annunciation also appears with a Visitation on a diptych in the Victoria & Albert Museum;[1] it was clearly a means of reducing the subject in order to conflate it with a second scene. The representation of St John in the Crucifixion is remarkable, if he is to be identified as the older man with a covered head.[2] The dorse of the panel bears the name 'Ludovicus' and the text 'omnis ? amo debet ? removi' (16th century ?) and crude renderings of a face and (?) a woman.

Provenance. Mayer collection by 1867.

Maskell, pp.173–4; Gatty 50; Nelson II, no.XII; BFAC 111; Koechlin 293; *LI* 36; *MRT* 119.

---

1   Longhurst, *Catalogue* II, pl.XIII, no.6824–1858.

2   If this figure is not St John, then it is remarkable that a mourner is depicted in his place. For an ivory writing tablet showing another Coronation scene with angels censing and holding a cloth of honour, see Randall 315.

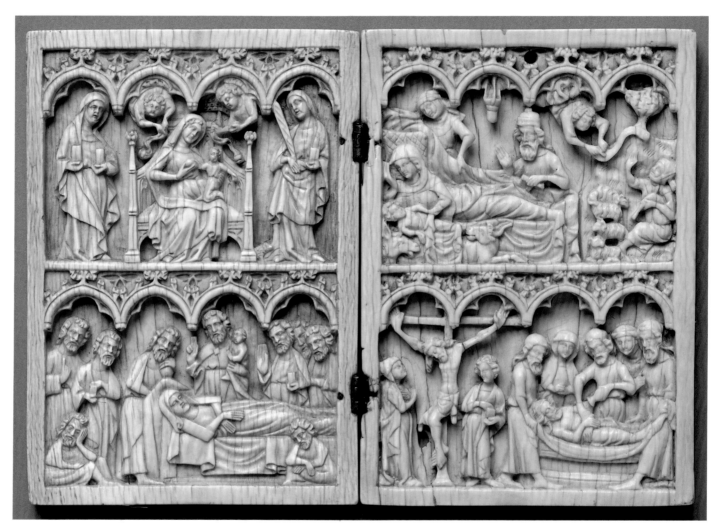

Plate XXX
Diptych of the Life and Passion of Christ; Dormition and Virgin enthroned

30

Diptych of the Life and Passion of Christ; Dormition and Virgin enthroned

1340–60   Flemish

M 8056

Pl.XXX

Ivory. 132 × 178 × 9 mm.

Two hinges.

Two registers. Scenes of the life of Christ and of the Virgin: *upper R*, 1. Nativity, with midwife about to place cover over Virgin, lamp hanging from roof, Joseph seated, wearing a hat, with a cane; 2. Announcement to a Shepherd, with bagpipe; *lower R*, 3. Christ on the Cross, with Mary and John; 4. Entombment, with one figure anointing the body; *lower L*, 5. Death of the Virgin, with Apostles mourning and God the Father or Christ blessing, holding her soul as infant; *upper L*, 6. Virgin enthroned, holding orb, with Child kneeling reaching for it, between censing angels; at each side, a woman (L) in wimple, holding two books, (R) with book and palm branch. Each scene is in an architectural canopy of four rounded trefoiled arches decorated with finials and crockets.

The chronology of this diptych begins exceptionally in the upper right panel and reads clockwise down and around to the upper left. The scenes are related to each other thematically and visually by the presence of a recumbent figure in three, and the carver seems interested in rendering drapery, indeed allowing considerable space for these prone figures (the Crucifixion is squeezed to allow for the Entombment). Little attention is given to the Apostles, and they seem ill-worked by contrast. Iconographically the scenes are notable for the presence of a female figure in the Nativity (the entire scene is related to Koechlin 343, 354, 460 and 465, all second half of the 14th century) and for female saints rather than angels in attendance on the Virgin (scene 6). These features raise the possibility that the diptych was commissioned by a woman. The female at R may be a second reference to the Virgin, who is depicted in the Ascension at this period with palm and book; and the figure with two books may be St Clare or the Virgin's mother, St Anne, who taught her to read. The laying-out of the Virgin in the Death scene resembles that in Koechlin 295 and 519. As much as any other panel in the collection, this diptych shows that the selection and placement of scenes, however conventionally each was rendered, gives the final work the air of a unique creation.

Provenance. Mayer collection by 1867.

Gatty 51; Maskell, p.173; Nelson II, no.XIII; BFAC 124; *LI* 41.

Plate XXXIa
Diptych of the Virgin and Child; Crucifixion

31

Diptych of the Virgin and Child; Crucifixion

1350–75   French

M 8007

Pls XXXIa–b

Ivory. 88 × 55 × 10 mm. (each panel)

Traces of gold on Christ's perizonium and hair; traces of red pigment on the palms of his hands and in the wound on his R side. Two hinge-marks.

Left leaf. Virgin standing, holding Child with small (?) orb on L arm and an unidentifiable object (perhaps the end of a flowering branch, now broken) in R hand; on each side, an angel with a taper. *Right leaf.* Christ on a Dry Cross, with John, holding book at L, and Virgin, with book at R; sun (L) and moon (R) above. On each panel an architectural canopy of three gothic arches inset with trefoil tracery, with finials and crockets, above which a band studded with small orbs.

The iconography of the Virgin and Child is entirely conventional, as is the joining of the subject with that of Christ on the Cross. The latter scene is notable for its reversal of the standard placement of Mary and John. The Crucifix, with the standard orientation of Christ slumped to his R, demonstrates that the artist cannot have been working from a mirror image of any kind; the cause of the reversal of the other figures is obscure. These two subjects, or a Christ on the Cross with a Coronation of the Virgin, are also frequently found together in two registers of the central panel of a triptych. Such juxtapositions give the Virgin a pictorial status virtually equal to that of Christ and reflect contemporary interest in Mary as a human image in her own right. This type of Virgin scene appears with a Crucifixion on three pieces in the Walters Art Gallery: in a diptych by the Master of the Berlin triptych of the third quarter of the 14th century, and on the backs of two crozier-heads of *c.*1340–50.[1] Drapery on the central figures is rendered as a group of semi-circular folds below the waist with a broad open drop below. The Cross as a Dry Tree is relatively uncommon.

Provenance. Fejérváry collection by 1855.

Henszlmann 677; Pulszky 51–2; Westwood 431 and 427 ('73.161 and '73.158); Gatty 47; Nelson II, no.XIV; BFAC 126; *LI* 40.

Plate XXXIb
Crozier-head, showing Virgin and Child with angels.
Walters Art Gallery, Baltimore

1   See respectively Randall 301 and (the crozier-heads) Randall 286 and 287. The first crozier-head, Walters Art Gallery 71.231, is our Pl.XXXIb.

Plate XXXIIa
Left panel of a diptych, with six scenes of Christ's Passion

32

Left panel of a diptych, showing six scenes of Christ's Passion

Third quarter of the 14th century   French

M 8057

Pls XXXIIa–b

Ivory. 206 × 127 × 11 mm.

Plate XXXIIb
Diptych of Christ's Passion, formerly in Vich cathedral.
Walters Art Gallery, Baltimore

Two hinge-marks at R.

Three registers. Scenes of the Passion: *upper*, 1. Entry into Jerusalem, with Zachaeus in tree and man spreading his cloak; *middle*, 2. Garden of Gethsemane, with all Apostles, two with hands to head in sleeping posture; 3. Betrayal, with Jew and two tormentors in winged head-dress (see also No.35), with clubs; *lower*, 4. Christ on the Cross, with Mary and John; 5. Descent; 6. Entombment, with Joseph of Arimathea anointing Christ's body. Each register surmounted by an architectural canopy of four trefoiled arches decorated with finials and crockets; no decoration in spandrels; a band of small orbs along the R vertical frame.

Koechlin groups this panel with three other ivories stylistically and iconographically allied with a mid-14th-century diptych (814) formerly in Vich, Catalonia and now in Baltimore (Pl.XXXIIb).[1] Each register of the Vich piece contains at least two scenes, whereas in the Liverpool panel the first scene of the first register is expanded to fill the entire upper space.[2] Having lavished space and added figures relative to the Vich model for the Entry, our artist was forced to compact three scenes into the lowest register. The renderings are animated but largely conventional. The Betrayal is, however, interesting for the presence of three tormentors (called 'rare' by Koechlin), who anticipate the next stage of Christ's Passion. Their elongated clubs or staves had become standard attributes for villains of various kinds (e.g. Goliath), at the same time as they are used innocuously with shepherds and figures of Joseph. The winged head-dresses are pagan in origin, adapted by medieval craftsmen as a sign of evil.[3] Whatever the quality of their renderings, artists working in commercial circumstances depended on the repetition of stock gestures

and figures; here compare Judas in the Betrayal and Joseph of Arimathea in the Descent. As Randall noted, 'This leaf is probably by the same hand' as the diptych from Vich. The complete Liverpool diptych must have looked much like the Vich diptych, if not in every detail. There the Entombment is placed in the lowest register of the R leaf; in the Betrayal scene the Christ figure and one of the tormentors are omitted, and the model used in the Liverpool panel for Judas is used as Christ. That the Vich L panel is narrower accounts for the reduction in figures in both the Entry and the Betrayal scenes; but the fuller complement of figures in the Liverpool piece suggests that its design and production preceded that of the Vich diptych. Another point at which the Vich leaf is not an exact match to the Liverpool panel is the lack of beading on its frame.

Provenance. Mayer collection by 1855.

Guardbook no.72b; Maskell, p.173; Gatty 48; Nelson II, no.XVI; BFAC 113; Koechlin 815; *LI* 39; Randall 299.

---

1   Walters Art Gallery, 71.179; Randall 299 and colorplate 74.

2   It is difficult to know whether this enlargement of the Entry reflects an interest of the artist or of the patron in the subject, or whether it was a convention with regard to this subject: see Randall, 299–300.

3   R. Mellinkoff, 'Demonic winged headgear', *Viator* 16 (1985), pp.367–81, at p.380, note 71.

Plate XXXIII
Left panel of a diptych, showing the Virgin and Child with SS Peter and Paul

33

Left panel of a diptych, showing the Virgin and Child with SS Peter and Paul

Mid-fourteenth century   French

53.114.277

Pl.XXXIII

Ivory. 109 × 71 × 7 mm.

Two deep hinge-marks at R edge; chisel marks on L edge.

Virgin and Child, standing, the former holding the Child, who has an apple or orb, on her L arm, and a book in her R hand; at L, St Peter, as younger man, with book and elongated key; at R, St Paul, bearded, with book and down-turned sword. Architectural canopy of three Gothic trefoiled arches decorated with crockets and finials on a triangular mounting or gable.

The subject of the Virgin and Child between saints, as noted under No.27, is relatively rare; for more examples, see Koechlin 52, 825. These saints also occur occasionally beside a Coronation of the Virgin (Koechlin 209A, 218); their representation, as transmitters of the Word, beside the Virgin is further evidence of her increasing importance in the period. The artist gives animation to an essentially static scene through the long flow and variation of drapery, one of the robes ending in zig-zag folds. St Peter is usually represented as an older man, and this figure is particularly noteworthy as the head, with distinctive features and jug-handle ears, appears to be a 'portrait'. Paul's sword, a symbol of his martyrdom, is sheathed or wrapped in an unusual manner. The panel probably faced a Crucifixion.

Provenance. Philip Nelson (*ob.*1953).
LI 54.

34

Left panel of a diptych, showing the Virgin and Child with SS John the Baptist and Katherine

1350–60   South German

53.114.278

Pls XXXIVa–c

Ivory. 94 × 64 × 8 mm.

Virgin and Child 'lactans'. Virgin standing, crowned with a short veil beneath; *L*, St John the Baptist, standing, with a long gown of skins and a covering mantle, holding a roundel with image of the Agnus Dei; *R*, St Katherine, crowned with a short veil beneath, holding palm and wheel. Architectural canopy of three Gothic trefoiled arches, surmounted by a triangular frame with crockets and finials at the apex. Unidentified coat of arms, presumably south German: in L spandrel, a cross; in R, a lion rampant, *queue fourchée* (no colour).[1] The R leaf is a Crucifixion panel, formerly Kofler-Truniger S85 and now in a private collection (Pl.XXXIVb).

The workmanship of this panel is undistinguished, apart from the fine deep folding of the Virgin's gown and the imbalance in the design of St Katherine's. The female facial types are characterised by receding chins and sweetness of expression. The extreme bent heads, slightly bowed posture, and broken stance of the left legs indicate a movement towards the style of the fourth quarter of the century. The iconography of the Virgin nursing the Child is another aspect of contemporary emphasis on the humanity of Mary, as is her intense gaze at the infant. Although the saints were probably selected by the patrons, we may refer to two other instances of SS John the Baptist and Katherine beside the Virgin: Glasgow, Burrell Collection, 21 / 9 (Pl.XXXIVc: *Gifts*, no.11; not known to Koechlin) and Épinal, Bibliothèque Municipale, MS 201 (Koechlin 587).

Provenance. Philip Nelson (*ob.*1953).

P. Nelson, 'A French armorial ivory of the fourteenth century', *THSLC* 101 (1949), 63–4; *LI* 53; H. Schnitzler et al., *Mittelalterliche Elfenbein- und Emailkunst aus der Sammlung E. und M. Kofler-Truniger, Luzern* (Düsseldorf, 1965), no. S85; *Rarer Gifts than Gold: fourteenth-century art in Scottish collections*, The Burrell Collection 28 April – 26 June 1988 (Glasgow, 1988).

---

1   The arms should be identified neither with those of Sir Bartholomew Burghersh (Nelson), nor with those of Bishop Grandisson of Exeter (Schnitzler). Grandisson's arms feature two eagles and a mitre.

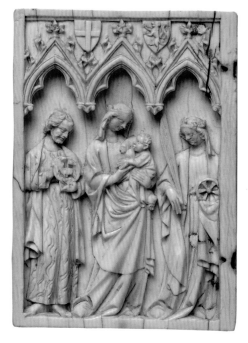

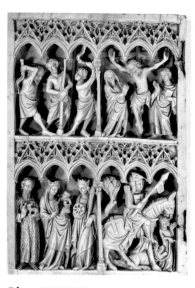

Plates XXXIVa–b
Diptych showing (left) *the Virgin and Child with SS John the Baptist and Katherine and* (right) *the Crucifixion.* The right panel is in a private collection

Plate XXXIVc
Left panel of a diptych, including (bottom left) *the Virgin and Child with SS John the Baptist and Katherine.*
Glasgow Museums and Art Galleries: the Burrell Collection

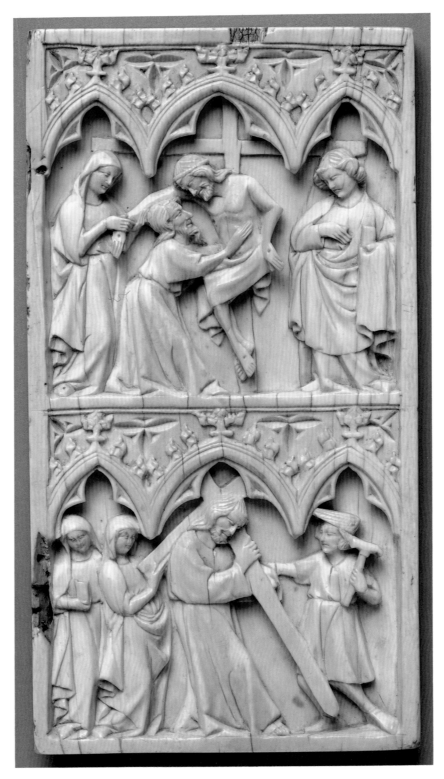

Plate XXXVa
Right panel of a diptych, showing two scenes from the Passion

35

Right panel of a diptych, showing two scenes from the Passion

1350–60   French

M 8004

Pls XXXVa–b

Ivory. 200 × 105 × 11 mm.

An exceptionally heavy piece. Two hinge marks on L edge.

Two registers. Scenes of the Passion: *below*, Christ bearing the Cross, with two Maries behind, one with a book, the other supporting the cross-bar, and with a tormentor ahead, holding a hammer and wearing a winged head-dress; *above*, Descent from the Cross, with Joseph of Arimathea supporting the body and Mary holding Christ's arm and John with book. On each register an architectural canopy of three Gothic trefoiled arches decorated with leafy crockets and finials, with a trefoil design incised in the spandrel, of which the central arch is larger.

Plate XXXVb
The complete diptych, the left panel in the V & A. Courtesy of the Board of Trustees of the Victoria & Albert Museum, London

The L panel survives in the Victoria & Albert Museum (Pl.XXXVb), having scenes of (below) the Flagellation and (above) the Crucifixion.[1] The complete piece thus reads across the bottom of both panels and across the top, forming four stages of the Passion. The tormentor with hammer does not strictly belong in the Bearing scene, but by this device the artist (and others who use the theme; see e.g. Koechlin 58, 176, 282, 358, 819, 833) has in this figure both indicated and fulfilled the next traditional scene of the Nailing to the Cross. This kind of pictorial conflation must have been a response to the limitations of the medium and the demands of any given commission. The significance of a winged head-dress is noted at No.32. The figure of Joseph of Arimathea is another instance of the stock posture used in No.32. The semi-circular rendering of Christ's arm supported by Mary is graceful but not unknown elsewhere (Koechlin 220, 236, 286, 819, 833). It can be found in manuscript painting as well; see, for instance, scenes of the Passion in an English Psalter now in Trinity College, Cambridge.[2] Prior and Gardner (pp.378–9) compare the Victoria & Albert panel to an alabaster tomb at Westminster.

Provenance. On dorse, 'Dominus Willelmus Lidiat' (14th century), perhaps of Lydiate Hall, south-west of Ormskirk (Lancs). Lydiate is a parish with a long recusant tradition; four alabaster carvings of the life of St Katherine still survive as local treasures: N. Pevsner, *Lancashire: 2 the rural north* (Harmondsworth, 1969), pp.171–72. Fejérváry collection by 1855.

Henszlmann 679; Pulszky 56; Westwood 411 ('73.146); Gatty 58; Maskell, p.173; *Victoria County History of Lancashire* III (London, 1907), pp.200–8; Nelson II, no.X; E.S. Prior and A. Gardner, *An Account of Medieval Figure-Sculpture in England* (Cambridge, 1912); BFAC 108; Koechlin 290; Longhurst, *Catalogue II*, p.18, fig.1; *LI* 35.

---

1   London, Victoria & Albert Museum, 161–1896: Longhurst, *Catalogue II*, pp.18–19, pl.XIII.

2   MS O.4.16 (mid- to late 13th century and early 14th): L.F. Sandler, *Gothic Manuscripts 1285–1385*, A Survey of Manuscripts Illuminated in the British Isles 5 (London, 1986), no.14, fig.33. A tormentor in winged headgear is just above in the road to Calvary scene.

Plate XXXVI
Left panel of a diptych, showing
SS John the Baptist, Christopher
and James the Greater

36

Left panel of a diptych, showing SS John the Baptist, Christopher and James the Greater

1390–1400   ?Flemish

M 8003

Pl.XXXVI

Ivory. 78 × 52 × 6 mm.

Two hinge-marks. The borders are broken or worn on three sides, with part of the figure of St John lost; and one serious crack extends from the lower frame to mid-panel.

Three standing figures of saints. Left, St John the Baptist, in animal-hide gown with mantle knotted loosely below the waist, gesturing at an *Agnus Dei* in his left arm; *middle,* St Christopher, in waters, with staff, bearing the nimbed Christ Child, who is holding an orb and blessing; *right,* St James the Greater in a long gown and tall hat, holding spiked staff and book, and wearing a scrip with shell across the shoulder. Architectural canopy of three trefoiled arches, each surmounted with a triangular gable with crockets and a finial, the pediments and spandrels having a similar cut-out trefoil design.

Images of the saints carved as objects of devotion in their own right, apart from scenes of the life and Passion of Christ or the Life of Mary, presage a new period, in which the latter were not less honoured but the saints more elevated as individual intercessors. The figures are elongated to fill the pictorial space and are conceived in a more rigid, angular manner, by contrast with the softer, flowing lines of figures of the high period of the 14th century. The three facial types are all similar, and the hair deeply incised. The craftsmanship is mediocre. The effect of a row of saints, unrelated thematically to one another, is analogous to a litany and different in effect from the saints who stand like sentinels on each side of the Virgin.

Provenance. Fejérváry collection by 1855.

Henszlmann 676; Pulszky 57; Westwood 490 ('55.41); Gatty 53; BFAC 132; *LI* 43; *MRT* 122.

37

Panel showing Christ with Instruments of the Passion; Nativity and Annunciation to the Shepherds

Second half of the 14th century, or 19th century   ?German

53.114.281

Pl.XXXVII

Ivory. 86 × 63 × 6 mm.

Plate XXXVII
Panel showing Christ with Instruments of the Passion; Nativity and Annunciation to the Shepherds

Several deep cracks in both upper and lower registers. The panel may have been broken in pieces and glued together again; some evidence of adhesive on the surface, in the background areas. Its authenticity is in doubt.

Two registers. Nativity and Christ in Judgement: *lower*, 1. Nativity, with Virgin holding arm of Christ Child, Joseph beside gesturing, with ? the handle of a cane; 2. at rear, Announcement to the Shepherds, as standing angel with scroll with standing shepherd with staff; at L another shepherd lying on hill with sheep; *upper*, Christ seated, wearing Crown of Thorns, his torso exposed, displaying wounds; on each side, an angel with Instruments of the Passion (L, a spear and ? nails, and R a cross). Kneeling figures, both in attitude of prayer: (L) a crowned woman with drapery falling from beneath the crown to ground; (R) a bearded man in nondescript drapery. On each register an architectural canopy of three trefoiled arches, with larger central arch, crockets, horizontally spread finials, with trefoil design incised in spandrels.

Lasko suggests that this panel may be German. If this is so, the artisan, whose workmanship is not refined, has nevertheless followed French iconography and settings. Although identified as donors (Lasko), the two kneeling figures are more likely to be the Virgin, typically dressed in crown and veil or drapery, and an Apostle (the flowing, nondescript robes are not those of a secular figure).[1] In 14th-century French ivories the scene of the Nativity is often conflated with that of the Announcement to the Shepherds, and a sense of distance achieved by reducing the size of the figures. It is less common to find the angel depicted standing beside the Shepherd (see however Koechlin 348bis). The juxtaposition of the two scenes in the diptych is also unusual, as are the kneeling figures. The middle arch is broader in the manner of French work of the first quarter or half of the century (Koechlin 348bis). The upper scene may be compared with the R leaf of a diptych in Lyons cathedral (Koechlin 524), and with the upper R section of a diptych in the Metropolitan Museum of Art, New York (Koechlin 234). These are both of the first quarter or half of the 14th century.

There is a real possibility that the Liverpool panel is a 19th-century work based on medieval models. In addition to the unusual iconography just mentioned, note that the animal by the crib looks much more like a dog than an ox or an ass. The carving lacks definition, and the panel itself lacks a purpose: it has neither hinge-marks, as for a diptych, nor the recessed back that identifies a writing-tablet.

Provenance. Philip Nelson (*ob.*1953).
LI 56.

---

1   For kneeling figures of the crowned Virgin, John, and angels with some Instruments see Koechlin 265, 276, 348bis, 775.

Plate XXXVIIIa
Writing tablet, showing the Crucifixion
(reverse)

Plate XXXVIIIb
Writing tablet (obverse)

38

Writing tablet, showing the Crucifixion

1390–1400   Northern French or Mosan

53.114.280

Pls XXXVIIIa–c

Ivory. 90 × 51 × 3 mm.

Crucifixion, with (L) Mary supported by a woman and (R) John, with book; behind, head of a Roman official (?Pilate). Architectural canopy, over one third of the height of the tablet, composed of three rounded arches with trefoiled edges, each surmounted by a tall gable with crockets and finial; inset of an elongated trefoil design in the spandrels.

This scene is on the dorse side of a utilitarian object meant to be used and reused for writing, while the decorated side could be used for devotional purposes. The recto – or writing side – is a chiselled-out rectangle divided vertically by a reserved strip forming two spaces suitable for writing in columns. The spaces would be filled with soft wax, which, when hardened, was written on with a metal stylus. The wax could be scraped over or discarded, when the text was no longer needed. On the dorse the posture of the Virgin collapsing in another Mary's arms, her elbows bent outward in a gesture of grief, derives from French work as early as the second quarter of the 14th century (Koechlin 292, 293 [= our No.29], 315, 348bis).[1] John's gesture of his hand to the side of his face is a standard iconographic sign of grief. A finer instance of the same iconography, with the turned head of the Roman official above John's L shoulder, may be seen in a diptych panel in Baltimore (Pl.XXXVIIIc);[2] the Virgin's drapery in the Liverpool panel may be a misunderstanding of the twisted skirt that was apparently originated by the master of the Baltimore diptych. The elongation of the figures is perhaps a response to the height of the pictorial space rather than to stylistic dictates, but this is a utilitarian object of relatively late date and correspondingly crudely worked.

Plate XXXVIIIc
Right panel of a diptych, showing Crucifixion with Roman official standing to the right. Walters Art Gallery, Baltimore

Provenance. E.L. Paget collection 155; Philip Nelson (*ob.*1953).

LI 55.

---

1   This posture was also common later: cf. Randall 297, 301, 306, 307, 314, and the Grandisson panel in London (*Age of Chivalry: art in Plantagenet England 1200–1400*, ed. J. Alexander and P. Binski, exhibition catalogue (London, 1987), 593). The arms are sometimes rendered in a virtually impossible gesture (Randall 314).

2   Walters Art Gallery 71.277 (Randall 303).

Plate XXXIX
Statuette of the Virgin and Child

39

Statuette of the Virgin and Child

Second quarter of the 14th century   French

M 8064

Pl.XXXIX

Ivory. 155 × 72 × 58 mm.

Traces of red staining survive in two folds on the back of the veil, and in the front folds on either side of the head. There are two serious cracks, over the L side of the Virgin's face, neck and across over her L shoulder, and from her waist down to the base on her R side; and there is general, light cracking. The small hole over the Virgin's brow on the veil may indicate the point of attachment of a filet or small crown.

Virgin 'lactans' and Child. The Virgin, who is seated, is depicted with head covered by a veil (no crown); the Child is clasping the breast with his R arm, and Mary's arm with his L hand. This statuette has a serene beauty that seems particularly suited to the medium of ivory. The Virgin's expression is alert but deeply content. Her drapery falls in realistic folds: two drops of the veil are pushed under others at the rear, and the folds become angular where displaced by her foot. The mantle falls back to expose her arm, forming a deep loop of material between her legs (a diagonal from her R shoulder, as noted by Koechlin), and the gown is somewhat rumpled where Christ's L foot poises on her knee. The artist deliberately contrasts the maternal stability and calm with a more agitated, angular rendering of the Child. His arms balance each other in opposing angles, his L leg turns at a right angle to his body, and he seizes from two directions at the breast. This posture appears to be unusual, though found in more rounded form on a few panels (Koechlin 621, 622bis). For all its Christian meaning, the statuette is also a finely-rendered moment between mother and nursing child; and the lack of crown, which is not unknown but infrequent, may emphasize this aspect. The humanity represented here is far removed from the iconic figures of earlier periods.

Provenance. Mayer collection by 1855.

Maskell, pp.174–5; Gatty 44; Nelson II, no.IX; BFAC 94; Koechlin 636; *LI* 37; *MRT* 118.

Plate XLa
Mirror case, showing an elopement

40

Mirror case, showing elopement

1320–40   Paris

M 8010

Pls XLa–b

Ivory. 132 × 127 × 9 mm. (diameter 170 mm.)

On the dorse, a lathe-turned hole in the centre and groove in the side frame to take the glass.

Chivalric romance scene, framed in an undecorated roundel. On a bridge: *left*, 1. four mounted knights in armour, one gesturing at the central tower; a pointed tower at rear with two women at windows; *middle*, 2. knight standing on the saddle of his horse, reaching up to help a young woman descend from a tower of the 'Castle of Love'; *right*, 3. three mounted knights, one with a young woman on his horse; all horses in ground-length trappings; *below the bridge*, 4. four

Plate XLb
Mirror case, showing an assault on the Castle of Love.
Walters Art Gallery, Baltimore

figures in a small boat: two lovers, a musician plucking a psaltery, and an oarsman. At each corner of the roundel, a bulbous grotesque with long, wavy ears and tail. These handles are an essential feature of a mirror case.

Rather than depicting a single moment (Maskell), this carving almost certainly represents a continuous narrative of four (not three: Koechlin) episodes: the knight arriving at the tower with his companions, the rescue or elopement from the castle, the lovers riding away on horseback, and the pair embracing to the music of love. The scene is, as Koechlin notes, harmoniously composed and finely rendered. The repetitive block pattern of the three architectural masses is broken by the flowing trappings of the horses, and the bridge is an ingenious device for sustaining three episodes at the same time as opening space for a scene below. The background trees are less skilfully fitted into the challenging circular pictorial space. Koechlin listed the subject of this mirror case as a variation of the theme of the 'Castle of Love'; no other surviving object is, however, iconographically similar to this one. Several caskets (see No.41; Koechlin 1285, 1293 and Randall 324) depict a river scene below an (apparent) elopement scene in two registers, and river scenes and elopements can be found separately (Koechlin 1164, 1312). A mirror case in Baltimore, Walters 71.169 (Pl.XLb: Randall 322), is widely considered to be by the same hand.[1] The relationship between mirrors and love, a commonplace since antiquity, is imaginatively exploited in both cases.[2]

Provenance. Fejérváry collection by 1855.

Henszlmann 673; Pulszky 48; Waring, p.24 (drawing); Maskell, p.174; Westwood 853 ('54.78); Gatty 65; Cust, p.149, fig.34; A. Maskell, *Ivories* (London, 1905), pl.xlviii.1; Nelson II, no.XV; BFAC 142; Koechlin 1105; Natanson, *Gothic* 46; *LI* 33; *MRT* 116; Randall 322; Gibson (1986).

---

1   The two mirror-cases differ in the rendering of armour and helms, which may indicate a different period of production.

2   D.W. Robertson, *A Preface to Chaucer: studies in medieval perspective* (Princeton, 1962), p.192, fig.59–63.

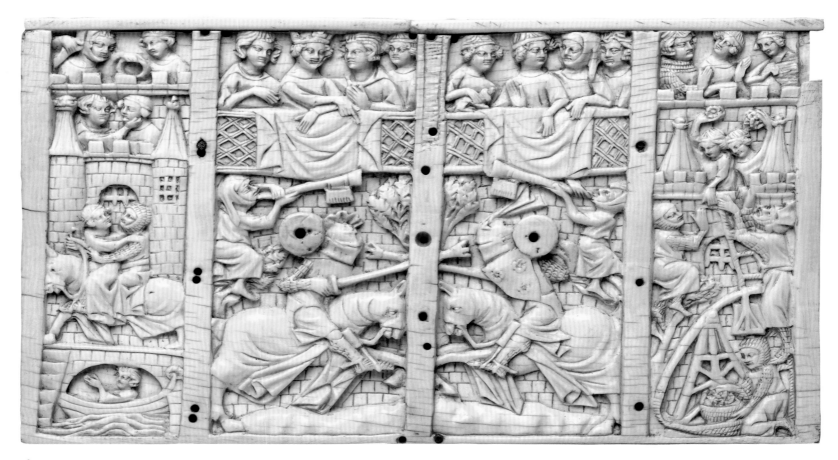

Plate XLIa
Casket lid, showing tournament with supporting scenes

41

Casket lid, showing tournament with supporting scenes

First half of the 14th century   French

M 8052

Pls XLIa–c

Ivory. 118 × 213 × 7 mm.

Two holes in raised discs of ivory (behind heads of the jousting knights) are the points of attachment for the (lost) metal handle. The three vertical bands show holes in varying sites where a decorated strip of metal was attached (Koechlin 1285), with hinges once attached at the top. The ivory strips along the upper edge are replacements, of a noticeably different colour, which conceal a broken piece at the centre.

Three scenes of chivalric romance, in four compartments. *L* (reading top to bottom): *Elopement*, 1. partial figures of lovers, man with unidentified object, woman with garland, behind crenellated wall; 2. second pair of lovers, with man making chin-chucking gesture, on crenellated tower with smaller side towers and portcullis below; 3. knight and lady, on horseback, crossing bridge, with steps to river; 4. under bridge, man in boat, presumably the oarsman waiting for the lovers. *Two centre panels*: *Tournament*, 1. on balcony, four partial figures in each panel, with drop of cloth at centre, including a crowned woman gesturing below, and a woman with a small dog; 2. two mounted knights in armour, with helms and crests, shield, and three-pronged lances, at full tilt; the shield, R, blazoned with three roses. At each side, a hooded man in a tree, blowing a trumpet (perhaps pages rather than heralds). *R*: *Storming the Castle of Love*, 1. behind crenellated wall, partial figures of a man in armour and two women; 2. at next level of crenellation, two women throwing roses at knights, who climb the wall by tree and ladder; 3. on the ground, a knight making ready to launch a basket of roses from a catapult. The diamond pattern of the balcony and the pieces of drapery (which call attention to the important figures) are conventional features of such scenes, as is the ashlar masonry.

Koechlin identified seven such caskets, all Parisian (Koechlin 1281–7), a group to which the Liverpool lid also belongs (Koechlin 1291). The lid of the lost Cracow casket (Koechlin 1285) is particularly close; while the Baltimore example (Pl.XLIb: Koechlin 1281) shows how the standard scenes could be switched round. The four side panels of the Liverpool casket, which do not now survive, would thus have shown quasi-Arthurian scenes, elephants and unicorns, and echoes of the romance of Alexander. An eighth casket (arguably not Parisian: Wixom, pp.123, 146) is now in the Cleveland Museum of Art (Pl.XLIc: not known to Koechlin). It, too, is closely related to the casket-lid in Liverpool (cf. Wixom, pp.124–5).

The charming scenes on this lid offer a further glimpse (see No.40) of the romantic and chivalric interests of the period. The military metaphors of assault and siege, with the pictorial images of crenellated walls, battlements, horses, arms, trumpets, weapons of war, seem to have been the poetry by which women were wooed and won; by the number of surviving scenes of this type in manuscript illustration and ivory carving made in commercial milieux, it was an analogy that worked.

Provenance. Mayer collection by 1855.

Guardbook 47a; Waring, pl.IV; Maskell, p.174; Gatty 67; J. Carter, *Specimens of the Ancient Sculpture and Painting now remaining in England*, 2nd edition by D. Turner, S.R. Meyrick and J. Britton (London, 1887), pp.146–7, pls cxiii–cxiv [closely similar casket, present location unknown]; Nelson II, no.XI, BFAC 138; Koechlin 1291; LI 34; *MRT* 117; W.D. Wixom, 'Eleven additions to the Medieval Collection', *Bulletin of the Cleveland Museum of Art* (1979), pp.86–151, at pp.110–26, 147–9; Randall 324–5; Gibson (1986).

Plate XLIb
Baltimore casket lid. Walters Art Gallery, Baltimore

Plate XLIc
Cleveland casket lid. The Cleveland Museum of Art, John L. Severance Fund, 78.39

42

Two panels from a casket lid, showing lovers in conversation

Third quarter of the 14th century   French

M 8008–9

Pls XLIIa–c

Ivory. 65 × 44 × 6 mm.; 64 × 45 × 6 mm.

Two panels, probably from a set of four, forming the lid (65 × c.180 mm.) of a casket in the same broad tradition as No.41. On each panel the side frames have three holes to mount them on a wooden base: note the correlation of the top holes on the R of the first panel and the L of the second. The dividing strip on each panel has three holes, at which a decorative metal strip was mounted. The handle was mounted partly on the R panel (see depression in central strip and hole to L) and partly on the next (lost) panel to the R. A complete example of such a lid may be seen in Boston (Pl.XLIIc: Museum of Fine Arts 64.1467; Calkins 79).

Four scenes of lovers. L, 1. young man, in long gown with hood, holding a hawk on gloved R hand, with L arm around young woman, holding small dog; 2. young woman chucking chin and holding garland over head of young man, the man touching her elbow; R, 3. young man, dressed as before, giving a garland to a young woman; 4. young man, holding a (?) hawking glove, chucking chin of young woman, who holds small dog. Background of stylized, snake-like trees; each scene under a rounded trefoiled arch decorated with crockets and finials.

The figures on these panels are conventional 14th-century representations of courting, with standard attributes; we have seen half-figures of this type in No.41. The garland, often represented as a simple ring, may have sexual connotations, as certainly do the predatory hawk held by the man and a small furry animal (often also in manuscript illustration a rabbit or cat) held by the woman. The glove may be identified by analogy with other such scenes (Koechlin 986, 988, 1187). Comparable scenes, involving the garland-ring, hawk, small furry animals and chin-chucking are reproduced in Koechlin, pls CLXXV–CLXXXIV, CXCV–CC, CCXIII–XV; Natanson, *Gothic*, 43, 45 (in which a hound is seizing a hare below the lovers), 47; Gaborit-Chopin 219 (garland-ring).

Plates XLIIa–b
Two panels from a casket lid, showing lovers in conversation

Plate XLIIc
Casket lid, showing courtship scenes. Theodora Wilbour Fund in Memory of Charlotte Beebe Wilbour: Courtesy Museum of Fine Arts, Boston

The work here is not particularly skilled, the tedious handling of drapery and the poorly-rendered trees standing as witnesses to the carver's ability.

Provenance. Fejérváry collection by 1855.

Henszlmann 674; Pulszky 49–50; Gatty 66; BFAC 140; *LI* 42.

43

Comb, showing Expositor and audience (obverse) and Fountain of Youth (reverse)

Early 15th century   French or Italian

M 8051

Pls XLIIIa–b

Ivory. 115 × 137 × 9 mm.

Frame and the edge of the scene itself missing at L and R; many of the tines of the comb missing or damaged.

Obverse. Expositor (far L) in outdoor pulpit addresses a boy (L) and five women. The young woman second from R holds a rosary. A sixth adult (far R) is now missing: see reverse. Narrow plain frame and plain background. *Reverse.* A young woman (far L), of whom only the arm now remains, takes the hand of a long-haired youth in a short tunic. They approach a fountain (centre) with animal-head spouts. The youth offers the girl a beaker of water. Narrow plain frame and plain background.

The scene on the obverse appears to be a *unicum*. On the reverse is the Fountain of Youth, a scene found in vernacular literature and art from the later 12th century onwards.[1] Here it closely resembles a comb in the Victoria & Albert Museum.[2] This relatively early type of comb has a plain frame and background, as distinct from the later type with an elaborate carved frame and a hatched background.[3] Both types exemplify the 'international Gothic' style, that was practised across Europe from Flanders to Italy.

Provenance. St Mary Magdalene, Ickleton (Cambs), a Benedictine nunnery. The north transept and an eastern chapel were demolished in 1791; it was presumably then that the comb came to light.[4] It was shown at the Society of Antiquaries 3 February 1803.[5]

Archaeologia XV (1806), p.405 and pl.xli; Guardbook 127; Gatty 69; Westwood 898–9 ('73.349–50); Maskell, p.174; BFAC 149; *LI* 44.

---

1 D.J.A. Ross, 'Allegory and romance in a medieval French marriage casket', *Journal of the Warburg and Courtauld Institutes* 11 (1948), 112–42, at pp.125–8.

2 London, Victoria & Albert Museum, 151–1879: Longhurst, *Catalogue II*, pl.lvi and p.68.

3 See London, Victoria & Albert Museum, 230–1867 and A.567–1910: Longhurst, *Catalogue* II, pl.l.

4 R. Radford, 'Ickleton Church', *Archaeological Journal* 124 (1967), pp.228–9.

5 'Craven Ord, Esq., F.S.A. exhibited to the Society a drawing which he had received from Thos. Walford Esq. F.S.A. of an antient comb, found in the ruins of Ickleton Nunnery, in Cambridgeshire, presented to the late Mr Shepherd, who resided in that neighbourhood, and now in the possession of his son': *Archaeologia* XV.405.

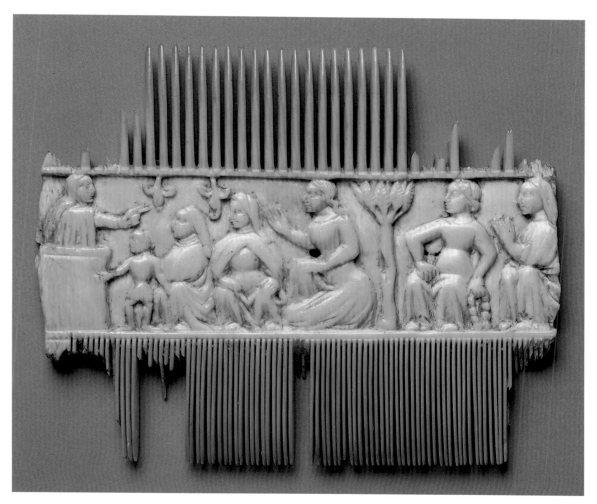

Plate XLIIIa
Comb, showing Expositor and audience (obverse)

Plate XLIIIb
Comb, showing Fountain of Youth (reverse)

6
Italian

With the few Italian pieces in the collection the wheel comes full circle, for they are multiple-copy bone panels, which are best compared with the Egyptian furniture-panels (Nos 2–4), and indeed also with the classicising casket-panels of 11th-century Byzantium (No.21). The term 'Embriachi' – which loosely designates them all – strictly applies to one Venetian workshop, which ceased to trade in 1406. Neither the earliest nor by any means the most productive, it was arguably the best. Certainly it did much to establish the canons of style and story in the caskets and mirror-cases of North Italy in the 15th century. These essentials of a lady's dressing-table show public taste at a modest and domestic level, far beneath the magnificence of the princely courts.

Plate XLIVa
Four bone panels, showing the Judgement of Paris

44

The Judgement of Paris

*c.*1400   Venice

50.129.1a–d

Pls XLIVa–b

Bone. Reading L to R: 113 × 31 × 11 mm.;
112 × 35 × 11 mm.; 113 × 34 × 11 mm.;
110 × 32 × 9 mm.

The panels are cut along the length of horse or ox bones; the backs are concave. The panel far L is chipped bottom L and has the top R corner detached.

The four panels were cut in Venice, in the workshop tradition of Baldassari degli Embriachi (*ob.*1406).[1] They are typical elements in a casket, showing the classical story of Paris in chivalric guise. In a landscape of trees the young Paris (R) stands beside the bearded shepherd Egylaeus, with staff, who had brought him up. Their cattle stand far L and centre L; Paris (centre R) makes his choice of Aphrodite in preference to Hera or Athena: cf.Pl.XLIVb.[2] Thus he obtains Helen of Troy as his wife. The story of Paris recurs in Embriachi, and Embriachi-related, material in a good number of European collections (von Schlosser).[3]

Provenance. Presented by the Committee of Gloucester City Museum in 1950.

J. von Schlosser, 'Die Werkstatt der Embriachi in Venedig', *Jahrbuch der Kunsthistorischen Sammlungen des allerhöchsten Kaiserhauses* 20 (1899), 220–82; Dalton 410; E.Merlini, 'La "Bottega degli Embriachi" et i confanetti eburnei fra Trecento e Quattrocento: una proposta di classificazione', *Arte Christiana* 727 (1988), pp.267–82.

Plate XLIVb
Paris makes his choice. Trustees of the British Museum, London

---

1   The choice of subject and the 'landscape' background favour an early date. The routine quality of the carving and the use of horse or ox bone suggest that the Liverpool panels are cheaper contemporary copies rather than products of the Embriachi workshop itself.

2   London, British Museum, MLA 85.8–4.12: Dalton 410.

3   One of the finest complete caskets is now in the Museo Civico, Catania: von Schlosser 27, fig.23. See also von Schlosser 8 (Bologna), 81 (Paris), 97 (Ravenna) and 124 (Vienna). For the total list of scenes in the Paris sequence see von Schlosser, pp.262–3, and pl.xxxviii (showing Paris's choice).

Plate XLVa
Five bone panels, showing Susannah and the Elders

Plate XLVb
Four bone panels, showing Susannah and the Elders

45

Susannah and the Elders

Mid-15th century   North Italy

53.114.282a–e; 53.114.283 ab, de

Pls XLVa–c

Bone. Nine panels, measuring: 64 × 32 × 12 mm each
(53.114.282a–e); 64 × 34 / 36 × 10 mm each (53.114.283 ab, de)

The panels are cut along the length of horse or ox bones: the
backs are concave. 53.114.282a and e are slightly chipped at
the bottom.

Casket panels such as were produced in commercial quantities throughout the 15th century, following the success of the
Embriachi workshop (No.44). These later panels are always
cut in bone, and they lack the landscape background that is
characteristic of the Embriachi tradition. Both groups here

illustrate the story of Susannah and the Elders (Daniel
13:1–64: Vulgate). Thus: (53.114.282, Pl.XLVa) (i.) Susannah
led away by a servant; (ii.) soldier in tunic and classical
armour, holding a club; (iii.) two soldiers hustle Susannah;
(iv.) Susannah protests her innocence; (v.) the two Elders are
bound to a tree and stoned. (53.114.283, Pl.XLVb) (i.)
Susannah leaves her house; (ii.) the bath in the orchard; (iii.)
soldier in tunic and classical armour, holding a club; (iv.) the
orchard.

The major omissions are the Elders spying and making their
false accusation; Susannah before the judge; and Daniel's
cross-questioning of the Elders, that shows they are lying.
The whole sequence may be seen in a casket in the British
Museum (Pl.XLVc).[1]

Provenance. Philip Nelson (*ob*.1953).

Von Schlosser, pp.222–33; Dalton 404; Merlini (cf.No.44), at
pp.275–7.

Plate XLVc
A complete Susannah casket. Trustees of the British Museum,
London

1   London, British Museum, MLA 78.11–1.20: Westwood, 703–6 ('58–
151.154); von Schlosser 52).

46

Four unrelated bone fragments

15th century   North Italy

53.114.283c; 50.129.3a–c

Pl.XLVI

Bone. Measures: 77 × 37 × 9 mm. (53.114.283c);
79 × 31 × 8 mm. (50.129.3a); 55 × 34 × 7 mm. (50.129.3b); 44
× 20 × 6 mm. (50.129.3c)

53.114.283c is in good condition. The other three fragments
are badly damaged.

(53.114.283c): the lute-playing satyr in a forest has been
wrongly incorporated in the second Susannah series (No.45:
53.114.283ab, de). He belongs to the range of forest imagery
with wild beasts and wild men. (50.129.3a): the second
fragment is from a Susannah casket, showing the two wicked
Elders tied up to be stoned. (50.129.3b): the third fragment
may be from yet another Susannah casket: e.g. a soldier in the
wooded garden apprehending Susannah. (50.129.3c): the
fourth fragment is beyond recall.

Provenance. The first fragment (53.114.283c) was acquired
with No.45 from Philip Nelson. The other three (50.129.3a–
c) were acquired at auction in 1950.

Von Schlosser and Merlini, as No.45 above.

Plate XLVI
Four unrelated bone fragments

47

Mirror-frame

15th century   North Italian

1986.227.2

Pl.XLVII

Bone. 445 × 275 × 20 mm.

Eleven panels set in an intarsia frame, one panel (far R) being slightly damaged.

Above. A long-haired youth with wings, perhaps blindfold, seated out of doors, holding in his R hand a rough staff and in his L hand an orb with a cross. A kneeling girl on each side, three trees and five large leaves. *Below.* Blank shields top centre. Seven panels with angels, of which two (far L and upper L) may have been supplied from another piece.

Arguably a marriage gift, for which the shields would be appropriately painted, the mirror has Cupid above and seven angels (two naked) below. The composition retains the classical flavour of the Embriachi tradition, without attempting so complex a story as Paris (No.44). The angels in particular are a recurring feature of such casket lids: Merlini (No.44 above), figs 4, 7, 9–12, 17, 19. The piece as a whole is a near-duplicate of a mirror-frame in Baltimore: Walters Art Gallery 71.92; Randall 354.

Provenance. Up Holland College (Lancs.); sold Christie's, 2 July 1986.

Von Schlosser; Randall.

Plate XLVII
Mirror-frame.
(Reduced)

Losses and Forgeries

i. Gothic ivories lost in May 1941:[1]

M 8001, M 8050, M 8058, M 8059, M 8066, M 8071, M 8073, M 8074, M 8076, M 8077. There is a 19th-century drawing of M 8076 (Pl. XLVIII). There is no reason to believe that any of these was other than genuine.

Plate XLVIII
19th-century drawing of the lost Gothic ivory, showing the Dormition of the Virgin

ii. Forgery in ivory:[2]

M 8068
The raising of Lazarus (Pl.XLIX): 19th century.
Distantly based on Goldschmidt I.102. Probably also a casualty of the fire in 1941.
Gatty 39; Graeven i.4.

Plate XLIX
The raising of Lazarus

iii. Forgeries in whalebone:

M 10040
Areobindus consular diptych (Pl.La): 19th century.
Cf. Volbach 13.
Henszlmann 663; Pulszky 34–5; Westwood 76 ('73.24);
Meyer 36; BFAC 249; Delbrueck, p.278; R.S. Bagnall,
Consuls of the Later Roman Empire, Philological
Monographs of the American Philological Association 36
(Atlanta, Georgia, 1987), p.547; *Byzance* 14.

Plate La
Areobindus consular diptych

M 10041
Philoxenus panel (Pl.Lb): 19th century.
Cf. Volbach 30, L panel.
Gori II.xv; Pulszky 1844, Roman 6, bought in Venice;
Henszlmann 661; Pulszky 33; Westwood 68 ('73.23);
Meyer 28; H. Graeven, 'Enstellte Consulardiptychen',
Römische Mitteilungen 7 (1892), 204–9; A. Maskell, *Ivories*
(London, 1905), pl.viii.3; BFAC 250; Delbrueck, p.278;
Bagnall, p.585; *Byzance* 18.

Plate Lb
Philoxenus panel

Plate LIa
Christ in Majesty

M 8015
Christ in Majesty (Pl.LIa): 19th century.
Cf. Goldschmidt-Weitzmann II.54.
Pulszky 1844, Byzantine 2, bought in Venice; Henszlmann 666; Pulszky 43; Westwood 181 ('58.94); BFAC 251; Maclagan, *Aréthuse* (note 4 below).

M 8072
Virgin and Child with Evangelists (Pl.LIb): 19th century.
Cf. Goldschmidt II.1.
Origin unknown: neither Fejérváry collection nor Guardbook List.

All four were displayed in the Burlington Fine Arts Club exhibition of 1923,[3] and all four confirmed as forgeries of the early 19th century by Eric Maclagan in the same year.[4] M 8072, which patently derives from Otto II's situla of 980,[5] was cut in Milan, as M 8015 may also have been. The consular panels, also Milanese, are by a different and superior hand. All four panels were casualties of the fire in 1941.

Plate LIb
Virgin and Child with Evangelists

---

1 See Introduction iii above.
2 See further Concordances below: Pulszky 66–8.
3 BFAC 249–52.

4 E. Maclagan, 'Ivoires faux fabriqués à Milan', *Aréthuse* i (1923), 41–3 and pls v–vi. This is effectively a French version of BFAC 249–52.
5 Goldschmidt II.1.

Concordances

i. The Fejérváry Collection.

In Henszlmann's 1853 exhibition catalogue of Fejérváry's collection as a whole (Henszlmann) the ivories lie within the sequence 641–92. Whereas in principle all these fifty-two items passed to Pulszky, six are renumbered (e.g. 656 = 25–6) and four new items, not listed by Henszlmann, were sold by Pulszky to Mayer. When the ivories reached Liverpool Museum, they were accessioned with the prefix M[ayer] and the subject matter 10 ('ancient') or 8 ('medieval'): thus the *Venatio* panel (No.7) is M 10042, the forty-second item in the 'ancient' section. (It will be noticed that the medieval sequence and part of the classical are the Pulszky numbers running in reverse.) Many of the 'ancient' items are outside the scope of the present catalogue: e.g. Henszlmann, nos. 641–5 are Etruscan, and nos. 646–55 are Roman. Others are lost or unidentifiable. Thus the list of fifty-one ivories that Mayer acquired from Pulszky (forty-seven plus the four not listed by Henszlmann) is reduced by twenty-five in the GATTY column (Gatty; Gatty, *Greek*; Gatty, *Egyptian*), and by a further five (four post-1500, one lost) in the present catalogue.

HENSZLMANN (1853)		PULSZKY (1856)	GATTY (1879–83)	GIBSON (1994)
641	Etruscan	4	M 10017	–
642		5	–	–
643		7	M 10019	–
644		8	–	–
645		–	–	–
646	Roman	9	–	–
647		2	–	–
648		12	–	–
649		–	–	–
650		21	–	–
651		20	–	–
652		10	–	–
653		11	–	–
654		3	–	–
655		24	–	–
656		25–6	M 10044	5–6
657		27	M 10042	7
658		23	M 10035	2
659[1]		–	–	–
660		29–30	M 10036	8
661		33	M 10041	losses and forgeries
662		32	M 10037	14

HENSZLMANN (1853)	PULSZKY (1856)	GATTY (1879–83)	GIBSON (1994)
663	34–5	M 10040	losses and forgeries
664	–	–	–
665	37	M 8021	10
666	43	M 8015	losses and forgeries
667	42	M 8016	25
668	40	M 8018	24
669	41	M 8017	13
670	44	M 8014	20
671	38	M 8020	19
672	45	M 8013	18
673	48	M 8010	40
674	49–50	M 8008–9	42
675	47	M 8011	27
676	57	M 8003	36
677	51–2	M 8007	31
678	53–4	M 8006	28
679	56	M 8004	35
680	55	M 8049 or 8056	29 or 30
681	36	M 8022	9
682	58–65	M 8032–9	21
683–92	69, 77, 70–1, 76, 73–4, 72, 85–6	–	post-1500
Pulszky adds:			
–	39	M 8019	16
–	66	M 8031	post-1500; dubious[2]
–	67	M 8030	post-1500; dubious
–	68	M 8029	post-1500; dubious

ii. The Mayer Collection

When he purchased the Fejérváry ivories, Mayer already had nine ivories of his own, including several of major importance. These all appear in the so-called 'Guardbook List', a brief hand-written census of ivory objects, which is now in the archives of the Museum.[3] In that this includes neither the Fejérváry ivories (1855) nor the little Anglo-Saxon Nativity (No.15) that came from W.H. Rolfe in 1858, it may be dated to pre-1855, apparently summarising Mayer's acquisitions over the previous twenty years. Two of these (Nos 11–12) came from the Possenti collection at Fabriano, that was gradually being dispersed in the mid-nineteenth century.[4] Another came from an archaeological context in England (No.43), as did Rolfe's Nativity. For Nos 29–30 there is no documentation.

Thus the conspectus of the Mayer collection as a whole is:

(a)   Guardbook list, pre-1855: 11–12, 17, 23, 26, 32, 39, 41, 43;

(b)   from Fejérváry, 1855: 4–10, 13–14, 16 (Pulszky), 18, 21, 24, 25, 27–8, 31, 35–6, 40, 42;

(c)   from Rolfe, 1858: 15, and M 8076 (lost: Pl.XLVIII);

(d)   unknown: 29–30.

iii. 'Fictile Ivories'

The Great Exhibition of 1851 brought it to general attention that casts could be made of the monuments of antiquity. Trajan's column – now in two sections at the cast court at the Victoria & Albert Museum – is a marvellous example of the genre. The technique could be extended to large bronze objects, as the doors and column at Hildesheim, and more cautiously to ivory panels. For these a new method was developed, using rubber solution rather than plaster of Paris, to reduce the danger of scratching or cracking the ivory.[5] Thus equipped, Edmund Oldfield and his colleagues made casts of some 400 ivories in museums and private collections throughout Europe. These 'Arundel casts' were offered to the public individually and in sets, in a tradition going back at least to the glass-paste Tassie gems of the late 18th century. In November 1855 a small exhibition was held in the Crystal Palace.[6] The South Kensington Museum was quick to recognise the value of this material, and from 1854 onwards bought casts from both the Arundel Society and from Elkington's of Birmingham.[7] An analytical survey of some 900 items in the South Kensington collection was provided by J.O. Westwood in his *Fictile Ivories* (1876).[8]

'Fictile ivories' permitted the scholarly comparison of items that were scattered across the museums and church treasuries of Europe. (They were, and are, much better than photographs.) They are a record of items that have been lost or destroyed; and occasionally they may permit a forger to perfect his art. For the present catalogue they concern the Fejérváry ivories only, most of which were cast before they were sold by Pulszky.[9] Ivories acquired by Mayer independently were never cast,[10] nor was the material that came to the Museum from other sources in the 20th century.

In the present catalogue the following items are available as casts. Westwood's numbering shows the year (e.g. '73 = 1873) by which they had been accessioned in the South Kensington Museum.[11]

GIBSON	WESTWOOD	ARUNDEL[12]	ELKINGTON
2	'73.12	–	✻
5	'54.45	Ia	–
6	'54.46	Ia	–
7	'54.49	IIa	–

GIBSON	WESTWOOD	ARUNDEL[12]	ELKINGTON
8	'58.4,5	IId	–
9	'55.14	IVc	–
10	'58.10	IVe	–
13	'54.60	Vn	–
14	'54.87	–	∗
18	'73.133	–	∗
20	'58.27	VIIh	–
24	'73.108	–	∗
25	'73.73	–	∗
27	'73.139	–	∗
28	'73.147–50	–	∗
31	'73.161	–	∗
35	'73.146	–	∗
36	'55.41	XIq	–
40	'54.78	XIIb	–
43	'73.349–50	–	∗

1   Cast, now lost, of consular diptych, of which the original is in the Domschatz, Halberstadt: Delbrueck, no.2; Volbach, no.35; Westwood 45–6 ('54.53,54).

2   For the assessment of Pulszky 66–8 I am indebted to the guidance of Dr Christian Theuerkauf of the Berlin Museums.

3   Guardbook I, p.90: three bifolia, numbered 1–5: fol.3ᵛ, 4ᵛ, 5ᵛ–6ᵛ blank; fol.6ʳ⁻ᵛ unnumbered. I am indebted to Margaret Warhurst for drawing my attention to the Guardbook List and to Susan Nicholson for help with its transcription.

4   The Possenti collection was dispersed at auction in Florence in 1880: Lugt 40035. Mayer's two Possenti ivories (Nos 11–12) were acquired long before that, as probably also was the related panel now in the Louvre (Goldschmidt II.9), and arguably also the Widow of Nain panel in the British Museum (Goldschmidt II.6; Pl.XIIId).

5   E. Oldfield, *Catalogue of Select Examples of Ivory-Carvings from the Second to the Sixteenth Century*, Arundel Society (London, 1855), p.3 (gutta percha impressions) *et passim*; cf. Westwood, pp.x–xi.

6   *Descriptive notice of the drawings, tracings, models and miscellaneous publications of the Arundel Society exhibited November, 1855, in the Crystal Palace, Sydenham* (London, 1855), pp.28–35.

7   A combined list of the Arundel and Elkington casts was issued by the 'Department of Science and Art of the Committee of Council on Education': *Reproductions of Carved Ivories – A Priced Inventory of the Casts in Fictile Ivory in the South Kensington Museum* (London, 1890).

8   J.O. Westwood, *A Descriptive Catalogue of the Fictile Ivories in the South Kensington Museum* (London, 1876).

9   'There are still two Ivories in your collection of which I should greatly desire to have casts made . . . namely nos.665 [no.10: Ascension] and <text damaged> in your catalogue. If you will kindly entrust the two ivories to me I will return them with all dispatch. I remain, dear Sir, yours very truly and already greatly obliged, J.O. Westwood': Westwood to Pulszky 9 February 1854 (Budapest Széchényi Library, VIII.1159).

10   The exception is No.43, which had been known in antiquarian circles since the beginning of the 19th century.

11   E. Oldfield, *A Catalogue of Specimens of Ancient Ivory-Carving in Various Collections* (London, 1856), bound with M. Digby Wyatt, *Notices of Sculpture in Ivory*, a lecture delivered to the Arundel Society 29 June 1855.

12   Arundel casts are numbered according to the catalogue of 1856; Elkington casts are marked with an asterisk.

Select Bibliography

Age of Spirituality	*Age of Spirituality: late antique and early Christian art, third to seventh century*, ed. K. Weitzmann, exhibition catalogue (New York, 1979).
Arundel casts	See Oldfield below, Wyatt below.
Beard	C.R. Beard, 'The Joseph Mayer Collections I', *The Connoisseur* 95 (1935), 135–8, 201–4.
Beckwith	J. Beckwith, *Ivory Carvings in Early Medieval England* (London, 1972).
BFAC	*Catalogue of an exhibition of carvings in ivory*, Burlington Fine Arts Club (London, 1923).
Byzance	*Byzance: l'art byzantin dans les collections publiques françaises*, Musée du Louvre 3 November 1992 – 1 February 1993 (Paris, 1992).
Calkins	R.G. Calkins, *A Medieval Treasury: an exhibition of medieval art from the third to the sixteenth century* (Cornell / Utica, 1968).
Cust	A.M. Cust, *The Ivory Workers of the Middle Ages* (London, 1902).
Dalton	O.M. Dalton, *Catalogue of the Ivory Carvings of the Christian Era . . . in the Department of British and Mediaeval Antiquities and Ethnography of the British Museum* (London, 1909).
Delbrueck	R. Delbrueck, *Die Consulardiptychen und verwandte Denkmäler* (Berlin / Leipzig, 1926–9).
Gaborit-Chopin	D. Gaborit-Chopin, *Ivoires du Moyen Age* (Fribourg, 1978).
Gatty	C.T. Gatty, *Catalogue of Mediaeval and Later Antiquities contained in the Mayer Museum* (Liverpool, 1883).
Gatty, *Egyptian*	C.T. Gatty, *Catalogue of the Mayer Collection I: the Egyptian, Babylonian and Assyrian Antiquities*, 2 edn (London, 1879).
Gatty, *Greek*	C.T. Gatty, *Greek, Etruscan and Roman Antiquities in the Mayer Museum, Liverpool* (Liverpool, 1883).

Gatty, *Prehistoric*	C.T. Gatty, *Catalogue of the Mayer Museum 2: Prehistoric Antiquities and Ethnography* (Liverpool, 1882).
Gibson (1986)	M.T. Gibson, 'Through the Looking Glass: a Gothic ivory mirror case in the Liverpool Museum', *The Chaucer Review* 21 (1986), pp.213–16.
Gibson and Southworth	M.T. Gibson and E.C. Southworth, 'Radiocarbon dating of ivory and bone carvings', *Journal of the British Archaeological Association* 143 (1990), pp.131–3.
Goldschmidt I–II	A. Goldschmidt, *Die Elfenbeinskulpturen aus der Zeit der karolingischen und sächsischen Kaiser* (Berlin, 1914–18, reprinted Berlin / Oxford, 1969–70).
Goldschmidt III–IV	A. Goldschmidt, *Die Elfenbeinskulpturen aus der romanischen Zeit* (Berlin, 1923–6, reprinted Berlin / Oxford, 1972–5).
Goldschmidt-Weitzmann I–II	*Die byzantinischen Elfenbeinskulpturen* (Berlin, 1930–4, reprinted Berlin 1979).
Gori	A.F. Gori, *Thesaurus Veterum Diptychorum*, 4 vol. in 3 (Florence, 1759).
Graeven	H. Graeven, *Frühchristliche und mittelalterliche Elfenbeinwerke in photographischer Nachbildung ser.1: aus Sammlungen in England* (Rome, 1898).
Henszlmann	E. Henszlmann, *Catalogue of the Collection of the monuments of Art formed by the late Gabriel Fejérváry of Hungary exhibited at the museum of the Archaeological Institute of Great Britain and Ireland* (London, 1853).
Joseph Mayer	*Joseph Mayer of Liverpool, 1803–1886*, ed. M. Gibson and S.M. Wright, Society of Antiquaries Occasional Papers, n.s.12 (London, 1988).
Kalavrezou-Maxeiner	I. Kalavrezou-Maxeiner, 'Eudokia Makrembolitissa and the Romanos ivory', *Dumbarton Oaks Papers* 31 (1977), pp.307–25.
Koechlin	R. Koechlin, *Les ivoires gothiques français*, 3 vol. (Paris, 1924).
Koehler	W. Koehler, *Die karolingischen Miniaturen* I–III, 3 vols. text and 3 vols. plates (Berlin, 1930–60).

Koehler – Mütherich	W. Koehler and F. Mütherich, *Die karolingischen Miniaturen* IV, text and plates vols. (Berlin, 1971).
Krzyszkowska	O. Krzyszkowska, *Ivory and related materials: an illustrated guide*, Institute of Classical Studies (London, 1990).
LI	*Liverpool ivories: special exhibition*, British Museum (London, 1954).
Longhurst	M.H. Longhurst, *English Ivories* (London, 1926).
Longhurst, *Catalogue* I–II	M.H. Longhurst, *Catalogue of Carvings in Ivory*, 2 vols, Victoria & Albert Museum, Department of Architecture and Sculpture (London, 1927–9).
Lugt	F. Lugt, *Répertoire des Catalogues de Ventes Publiques intéressant l'art ou la curiosité 1600–1900*, 3 vol. (The Hague, 1938–64).
MacGregor	A. MacGregor, *Bone, antler, ivory and horn: the technology of skeletal material since the Roman period* (Beckenham, 1985).
Maskell	W. Maskell, *A Description of the Ivories Ancient and Medieval in the South Kensington Museum* (London, 1872): Appendix, pp.165–75 (= the Liverpool Museum).
Meine Zeit	F. Pulszky, *Meine Zeit, mein Leben*, 4 vol. (Pressburg / Leipzig, 1880–3), = Hungarian *Életem és korom* (Budapest, 1880).
Meyer	W. Meyer, 'Zwei antike Elfenbeintaflen der k.Staatsbibliothek in München', *Abhandlungen der philosophisch-philologischen Classe der königlich bayerischen Akademie der Wissenschaften* XV.i (Munich, 1879), pp.62–84, pls I–III.
Morgan I–II	N. Morgan, *Early Gothic Manuscripts I 1190–1250, II 1250–1285*, A Survey of Manuscripts Illuminated in the British Isles 4 (London, 1982–8).
MRT	*Medieval and Early Renaissance Treasures in the North West*, exhibition catalogue (Manchester, 1976).
Mütherich	*Die karolingischen Miniaturen* V, text and plates vols. (Berlin, 1982).

Natanson, *Early Christian*	J. Natanson, *Early Christian Ivories* (London, 1953).
Natanson, *Gothic*	J. Natanson, *Gothic Ivories of the 13th and 14th centuries* (London, 1951).
Nelson I	P. Nelson, 'The mediaeval ivories in the Liverpool Museum I', *The Connoisseur* 25 (1909), pp.106–9.
Nelson II	P. Nelson, 'The mediaeval ivories in the Liverpool Museum II', *ibid*.30 (1911), pp.14–18.
PLRE I–II	A.H.M. Jones, J.R. Martindale and J. Morris, *The Prosopography of the Later Roman Empire* (Cambridge, 1971–80).
Oldfield	E. Oldfield, *Catalogue of Select Examples of Ivory-Carvings* (London, 1855).
Porter	D.A. Porter, *Ivory Carving in Later Medieval England 1200–1400*, State University of New York at Binghamton Ph.D. 1974 (Ann Arbor, 1986: University Microfilms International).
Pulszky 1844	Ivories in the Fejérváry Collection (handwritten list: see Introduction).
Pulszky	F. Pulszky, *Catalogue of the Fejérváry Ivories, in the museum of Joseph Mayer, Esq., F.S.A.* (Liverpool, 1856).
Randall	R.H. Randall Jr, *Masterpieces of Ivory from the Walters Art Gallery* (New York, 1985).
Randall, *Corpus*	R.H. Randall Jr. ed., *The Golden Age of Ivory* (New York, 1993).
von Schlosser	J. von Schlosser, 'Die Werkstatt der Embriachi in Venedig', *Jahrbuch der Kunsthistorischen Sammlungen des allerhöchsten Kaiserhauses* 20 (1899), pp.220–82.
Spätantike	*Spätantike und frühes Christentum: Ausstellung im Liebighaus Museum alter Plastik Frankfurt am Main*, 16 December 1983 – 11 March 1984 (Frankfurt am Main, 1983).
Strzygowski	J. Strzygowski, *Catalogue Général des Antiquités Égyptiennes du Musée du Caire: Koptische Kunst* (Vienna, 1904).

THSLC	*Transactions of the Historic Society of Lancashire and Cheshire*.
Vitali	L. Vitali, *Avori Gotici Francesi*, Museo Poldi-Pezzoli, Milan, April–June 1976 (Milan, 1976).
Volbach	W.F. Volbach, *Elfenbeinarbeiten der Spätantike und des frühen Mittelalters*, 3 edn (Mainz, 1976).
Waring	J.B. Waring, *Art Treasures of the United Kingdom: consisting of examples selected from the Manchester Art Treasures Exhibition, 1857* (London, 1858).
Weitzmann	K. Weitzmann, *Ivories and Steatites, Catalogue of the Byzantine and Early Mediaeval Antiquities in the Dumbarton Oaks Collection III* (Washington, DC, 1972).
Westwood	J.O. Westwood, *A Descriptive Catalogue of the Fictile Ivories in the South Kensington Museum* (London, 1876).
Wyatt	M. Digby Wyatt, *Notices of Sculpture in Ivory* (London, 1855).